CW00765706

FLYING LEGENDS

P-51 MUSTAN

John M. Dibbs

Text by
Stephen Grey

This book has taken me three years to put together and using photography from five years of shooting. A very special group of individuals and organizations have helped to realize this project. I owe thanks to Stephen Grey, a leading light whichever way you look at it. Everyone at Stallion 51, a very special place. Not only do individuals get to fly a TF-51 Mustang, the management of P-51s has led to a hangar full of the most beautiful aircraft. Lee Lauderback flew several of the featured '51s, with skill and rare ability. Lee's son, Brad, helped enormously. Tim Ellison flew me several times—once across the width of the United States! Cheers, Tim. Bud Anderson and Bob Goebel gave their time and are inspirational figures; it was an honor to work with the real McCoy!

Jeff Marchell was handed a challenge to fly and lead several photography missions and met it with skill and generosity. Anders Saether is a gentleman and was a huge inspiration to me, and with Bud Anderson, helped create warbird history. What a team! I would also like to single out Rachel A. Wisby for her enthusiasm, patience, and hard work that made the book possible. My wife Pam, my rock, whose business acumen made this book a reality. She is always there, dependable, funny, and caring. I also would like to thank Allan Burney for his support; and Bob Tullius; "The Duck," who rescued me a few times and proved a valuable and generous friend.

Thanks also to: Angela West, Candace Bennage, Charles Wise, Richard and Pete Lauderback, Charles Bonar, Anthony and Carol at Ranger Aviation in Kissimmee, Kevin Raullie, Art Vance, Kermit Weeks, Tony Banta, Jan Jonnson, Ken Ellis, Masa Ishizuka, Joe Newsome, Jack Roush, Gerri Montgomery-Prescott, John Hart, Robs Lamplough, Budd Davisson, Mark Wagner, Merle Olmsted, Bob Jepson, Tom Blair, Bill Hess, Brett Ward, The Imperial War Museum at Duxford, Mike George, Brad Hood, Bob Reese, Sam Sox, and Charles Osborn; there would be a lot of blank pages without you!

—*John M. Dibbs*

ACKNOWLEDGEMENTS

Photographic support: John Dickens at Pentax (UK), Peter Bowerman at CCS (Holdalls), and Graham Armitage at Sigma (UK).

Cameraship pilots:
Norman Lees, Jeff Marchell, Tim Ellison, Dave Stobie, Will Gray, John Romain, Chris Parker, Alan Walker, Brad Lauderback, and Andy Gent.

P-51 Pilots:
Dan Martin, Brian Adams, Dave Marco, Aubrey Hair, Brad Hood, Stephen Grey, Lee Lauderback, James Beasley Jr., Ed Shipley, Dan Vance, Vlado Lenoch, Al Shiffer, Pete Kynsey, Pete John, Ray Hanna, Andy Gent, John Romain, Pete McManus, Bud Anderson, Chuck Yeager, Gary Honbarrier, Bruce Guberman, Mike George, and Bob Tullius.

Text: Stephen Grey
Research: John Dibbs and Stephen Grey
Quotes compiled by: Tony Holmes and John Dibbs

Black and white images compiled by: Phil Jarrett, Sam Sox, Bill Hess, Merle Olmsted, and the 352nd Fighter Group Association via Alan Crouchman and John Dibbs.

Valuable information was 'cribbed' from the autobiography *To Fly & Fight* by Col. 'Bud' Anderson. www.cebudanderson.com

Book and design concept: John M. Dibbs/The Plane Picture Company

Prints available at www.planepix.com

First published in 2002 by MBI Publishing Company, 380 Jackson Street, Suite 200, St. Paul, MN 55101-3885 USA
© John Dibbs, 2002

Library of Congress Cataloging-in-Publication Data Available   ISBN 0-7603-1411-X

Edited by Amy Glaser   Printed in China

Their deeds may have passed, but we stand taller in the knowledge and consequence every day.

CONTENTS

Left: 334th Fighter Squadron, 4th Fighter Group, Debden, 1944.

FOREWORD

Col. Clarence E. 'Bud' Anderson

Most objective researchers would agree that the P-51 Mustang is probably the best all-around fighter that flew during World War II. Its great performance and long range made it unique. In the European theater the combat airplanes were all very close in direct comparison, but the Mustang was superior in many ways. In the areas that it was not the best, it was at least very competitive. It is one of the most popular fighters among World War II fans, and it is certainly my favorite for nostalgic reasons alone.

The Mustang has served me well. I had three different personal Mustangs named Old Crow, and during my two tours of combat in Europe, I flew 116 combat missions (over 480 hours) without a single abort or early return for mechanical problems or for any other reason.

World War II is pretty much remembered as a black and white world because there is very little color photography from that era. Thanks to the enthusiastic and dedicated men and women in the warbird community, there are many fine examples of these airplanes still flying today that allow us to see and hear the aircraft in all their glory. Many of these fantastic machines have been restored in historically accurate paint schemes and carry the markings of a particular Fighter Group or a particular pilot's own personal aircraft. There have been three different Mustangs painted like my World War II Old Crow. How lucky can one guy be?

Anders Saether of Oslo, Norway, painted his Mustang in the natural aluminum paint scheme of the 357th Fighter Group's, 363rd Fighter Squadron colors. His Old Crow was later repainted in a dark green, all-camouflage format. Mickey Rupp from Stuart, Florida, also painted his P-51 as the Old Crow in the natural aluminum paint scheme. This Mustang was later modified for air racing and repainted. Jack Roush from Livonia, Michigan, acquired a Mustang, and after a complete restoration, he also chose the 357th Fighter Group's fighting colors and Old Crow for a paint scheme.

I have had the honor and privilege of flying all three of these beautifully restored aircraft. These experiences have given me many nostalgic moments to recall World War II and the era I describe as the worst of times and yet the best of times of my life.

Amazingly, I never saw a Mustang until I arrived in the European combat theater. My entire fighter training was done in the P-39 Airacobra. We had heard about the P-51A and the A-36, but nothing about the P-51B and the marriage of the great airframe with the Packard-built Merlin engine until we got to England. The first Mustangs had just been delivered to the 354th Fighter Group of the 9th Air Force. They were on loan to the 8th Air Force for bomber escort until they were needed for the invasion of Europe. The Pioneer Mustang Group was so successful that the 8th Air Force demanded that they should be the next unit to receive the P-51. Fortunately, the 357th Fighter Group was next in line. Our unit records show that our first Mustang was delivered on December 19, 1943 and my log shows that I flew it twice that day.

The combat reports about the P-51's early success were widespread and we were eager to fly them. We had no flight manuals to study: It was a fast tour around the cockpit and a few words from someone that had at least flown a P-51 once, then you went up and tried out the Mustang. Surprisingly I have no distinct recollection of my first flight in a Mustang. The only explanation I have for not remembering something that should have been a highlight of my life was the situation at the time. I was a 21-year-old farm boy in a strange land and about to enter the uncertain world of aerial combat. Furthermore, I had just learned that my best friend had been shot down in a P-38 over Bremen, Germany, and was presumed dead.

I do recall that the Mustang was so much better than the P-39. The cockpit had a little more room and it flew like a dream. It had great performance at both high altitude and while flying 'down on the deck'. The P-51 was very agile and it gave you a lot of confidence. Its long range was a major performance factor no other fighter could match. My missions averaged over 4 hours, but the longest one was on D-Day when I logged 6 hours and 55 minutes and still had a good fuel reserve when I landed.

My most memorable combat encounter was in the spring of 1944. I was leading a flight of four 'B' model Mustangs on a bomber escort mission when we were attacked from above and behind by a flight of four Me109s. We turned into them and broke their attack and ended up in a large turning circle at about 30,000 feet. I could easily see the large intake of the left side of their engines that told me they were the high altitude models, the Me109G. We were at an optimum altitude for the Mustang too. Soon we started to gain on them in the turn. They straightened out and headed east back into Germany. The last Me109 started to climb but the three others flew level and made no turns. I sent my element leader and his wingman after the one climbing while I chased the other three with my wingman. Soon, I overtook the last man and simply moved into the six o'clock position and fired several bursts of my four 0.50 caliber machines guns. He started smoking badly and fell out of control. One of the remaining two rolled over and headed for the ground while the other made a sharp left climbing turn. We crossed over him and pulled up as steeply as possible. The Me109 reversed his turn and came after my wingman. I instructed my wingman to break off and to take evasive action while I covered him. The Me109 got right on his tail but I was now behind him and closing. He saw it immediately and made another sharp climbing turn. I crossed over his path and again climbed steeply, and traded my airspeed for altitude. The Me109 reversed his turn and now came after me. Looking back, I could see him over my left shoulder and saw that he was trying to follow my steep climb to get a shot. I pulled steeper and he tried to follow but stalled before I did. He rolled off on a wing and descended with me now about to get on his tail. Again, he came around in another hard climbing turn. This time the set up was a little different and I decided to try and turn with him. I didn't really want to be out there in front again. I lowered some flaps and pulled hard inside his turn. He saw this and reversed his turn and pulled up as steeply as he could. I raised the flaps, applied full power, and followed him in the climb. As soon as I got in range I fired a burst that caught him right in the center of the fuselage. He began smoking badly and slowly rolled over toward the ground; he was leaving a very long tail of thick smoke. I followed and watched as he dove from a very high altitude straight into the ground with a tremendous explosion. I got my flight back together and we re-joined the bombers. It had been an exciting day. This fight gave me great confidence in the Mustang. From a position of disadvantage, we had broken their attack and then shot down three out of the four enemy aircraft. The Mustang truly was a great combat fighter.

Above: Bud Anderson flying the Scandinavian Historic Flight's *Old Crow* over the former 357th FG base in Leiston, July 2001.

So just how do you capture the wild spirit of the Mustang on film? Many of you will be intrigued to learn how photographer John Dibbs produces such sharp, clear detailed photographs and what it is like to be photographed by him in-flight.

John is very thorough in pre-flight planning, and makes sure that everyone understands his objectives. He always uses a pilot that he is familiar with to fly the aircraft. I have been through at least three photo sessions with John, and feel well qualified to tell you what it is like in the air. Once airborne and joined up, I may have to fly a considerable time to get the desired environment. He is very picky! John then would signal me into the proper position for the photo and give me the hold signal. I would be flying formation, looking directly at John watching for signals and waiting for him to grab a camera and go to work. He would just sit there like a tourist, looking in all directions like the photos are the last things on his mind. When I first flew with John I was thinking 'Hurry up John, let's get this over with,' as I was working hard to hold the perfect position. All of a sudden John is a flurry of action, he is rapidly taking photographs, adjusting the lenses and even switching cameras. Then, it's all over. Once I saw the pictures, I was simply amazed; nothing had been left to chance. John's seeming indifference in the air is because the subject aircraft is only a small part of his creative equation. The results speak for themselves.

He certainly is an outstanding photographer as evidenced by the great photos in this book. His awesome sharp color photographs, blended with original images from that era, and the descriptive words of Stephen Grey, make this not only a great picture book, but also a fine work of World War II history. Thanks to John and Stephen, we can better appreciate these great machines and the men who flew them.

CE 'Bud' Anderson

–Col. Clarence E. "Bud" Anderson, USAF Retired

FOREWORD

Lt. Col. Robert J. Goebel

Immediately before World War II, the attempts by the United States to field a first-class fighter aircraft were very disappointing. The 31st Fighter Group was sent to England in June of 1942 (long before I became a member of it), their P-39 Airacobras were scheduled to follow shortly thereafter. The authorities of the RAF knew that this was folly and tactfully suggested that the aircraft be left in the states and that the RAF be permitted to equip the 31st with Spitfires instead. They did this and the 31st pilots continued to fly the Spitfire through the North African and Sicilian campaigns, and finally relinquished their beloved mounts in April of 1944. It must have been a humbling experience for the U.S. Army Air Force, especially because the returning American pilots praised the Spitfire as the best fighter in the world.

The British Air Ministry acceded to North American Aviation Company's suggestion that it be allowed to design a new fighter rather than become a second source for the manufacture of the P-40. The P-51, dubbed the Mustang, was the result, and what an aircraft! The final stroke—the pairing of the airframe to the Rolls-Royce Merlin engine—was indeed a match made in heaven.

The Mustang appeared in the skies over Europe just in time to save the daylight bomber offensive and became, arguably, the best fighter to come out of World War II.

The Mustang had it all. It was beautiful; even sitting on the ground it projected an image of power, speed, and character, which no other aircraft did. It had the

long legs necessary to cover the bombers to even the most distant of targets without the benefit of relays. Most importantly, it did this without giving up any performance advantage that it held over the best of the enemy propeller-driven fighters.

The admiration of the Mustang was not limited to Allied pilots. One of my victims over Ploesti, Romania, Lt. Herbert Franke who flew with JG-53, wrote a letter to his friend Ernst Pausinger who had been shot down and was in a hospital in Vienna. The letter, dated August 2, 1944, said: "Things again are rather mad. Deadly dogfights with large numbers of greatly superior Mustangs. We can scarcely get close to the bombers." He lived only 16 days after writing this letter, and sadly fell before the guns of my Mustang on August 18.

I knew of John Dibbs by reputation long before I met him. He had a reputation that placed him in the forefront of the World's leading aviation photographers. I believe that his talents are uniquely suited to capture the character of the Mustang on film. It is my hope that everyone, seeing this beautiful aircraft through the lens of John's camera, will be infused with the same passion for the aircraft as the young men who first took it into action so long ago.

Bob Goebel

–Lt. Col. Bob Goebel, USAF Retired

PREFACE

Stephen Grey

There are many authors who have described the Mustang's technical development and illustrious combat record. The specialist literature is immense and keeps growing. I have little to contribute to that story, so I shall communicate the magic of the Mustang flight. To those who dream, I hope to trespass your reveries and make the creative juices flow. To Mustang pilots—period or modernæI seek your indulgence.

I look to the sky, shaded from turquoise to indigo, framed by billowing white fair-weather cumulus. The freshly emerged sun outlines their voluptuous shapes with sparkling shades of rose and gold. The air is crystal clear, with a bracing westerly breeze.

Heavy with early morning dew, the dark green turf of Duxford spreads before me. Breathing deeply this mixture of oxygen and history, I find myself in profound contemplation, whilst gently rubbing the P-51's leading edge as if caressing the flanks of some willing thoroughbred.

The perfect compound curved cowling clothes the magic Merlin—its twelve exhausts protruding through symmetrical stainless shrouds. The spinner complements the cowl and smiley chin induction, dressing the union of four massive prop blades—neatly cuffed at the roots. A smooth, thin wing, beautifully blended to the elegant fuselage, the latter tapering to square-cut tail feathers. Every item, every rivet, every bracket, every opening, every space, and every component has a precise, well-crafted function; nothing is superfluous. Therein, lies its engineering elegance.

I touch, feel, pull, push, dip, examine, query, and shake off familiarity in the pre-flight walk-around. I stand back and wonder, yet again, how ingenious men crafted this engine of destruction, this mighty fighter, this thing of beauty, this illustrious bird of prey.

I climb, via the tire and spade door linkage, over the gun muzzles, onto the wing, and install myself with particular care in the cockpit of this rare razorback P-51B, with its tricky multi-piece canopy. Strapped in by parachute and seat harness, there is nothing in this relatively small but perfect space that I cannot read or reach except the glove I've just dropped. The cockpit is perfumed with a comforting and familiar smell of engine and hydraulic fuel and oils.

Antoine de St. Exupery, author and aviator, said, "I fly because it releases my mind from the tyranny of petty things."

I close my eyes and imagine the closeted briefing of a long time ago; the gut-wrenching greasy breakfast, the nervous jokes, and the nervous laughs. Thirty-six boys, from as many towns, await the signal to fire up 36 Mustangs, and in the name of freedom, set formation to the fight. Get a grip old boy. Shake off this musing. You need to be serious about flying this precious baby.

There is no other reason to delay, other than gently to prime, hit the starter and mags, and watch the sleeping giant burst into staccato life. After just three blades of rotation, a few puffs go past the cockpit and we have internal combustion. The engine smoothes to a sweet running idle, oil pressure rises, temperatures come off the bottom stops.

Above: Stephen Grey loops T.F.C.'s P-51C *Princess Elizabeth* over Duxford.

I fiddle with the birdcage canopy, and it finally locks—giving me a momentary prison-like sensation, whilst slightly muting the magic Merlin. I slide the side window and take in a breeze fanned by the prop; the air is mixed lightly with sweet smelling, crackling exhaust.

After a cryptic formal radio exchange, with chocks away and brakes checked, I start to gingerly weave whilst taxiing—all this despite no other traffic. A 180 into the wind at the holding point. Temperatures and pressures in the green; the engine bellows, aircraft strains at the brakes during run-up. Static checks fine, prop and mags checks excellent, idle is perfect. With radiator doors in manual, I re-run the cockpit drill—again, there is no reason to avoid flight.

The 24 center line is two degrees to my left, tail wheel locked. "Mustang cleared for take-off." No one is in front. No one is landing from behind. Stick aft of neutral, rightish rudder and aileron, throttle coming in firmly. Accelerating slowly, everything still "in the green"—the Merlin now singing its lusty song—3,000 rpm and 61 inches. The aircraft breaks ground in a three-point attitude and vibrantly comes alive. Stick in my right hand, throttle in my left, rudder firmly under my feet. A dab of brakes and a swift left hand to the gear lever, as the long shadows change size and shape and race us down the runway.

A clonk-clonk, followed by a lighter clunk, and the gear indicators switch from red to out. The theory of flight cannot equal its miraculous sensation—tons of exquisite machinery borne by the hand of man. Wings slice through the invisible liquid-like air. The ailerons, rudder, and elevator bite into a gentle climbing turn. Air speed rises fast, and the ground recedes. We shake off the chains of gravity, this beast and I. We shout a substantial silent shout of power and joy. We fly.

Fields are smaller. The sky stretches infinitely. We thread our way past pillars of bright clouds. A fleeting rainbow here, a passing shadow there—onwards and upwards. A wispy white tentacle snatches at the wing. Suddenly, we are above a

Above: North American Aviation's prototype P-51.

brilliant white quilt suspended in cobalt blue, and gently turn into the rising sun, with patches of green remote below.

I make a clearing turn and invert—no loose objects. Power up, nose down, stiffening controls—reveling in the freedom of flight. Surfing the immense undulations, I loop once, maybe twice. It is as if the aircraft is on rails. We rumble through our own wake. Sensations pulsing through fingertips, we convert energy into vertical, unload and roll in pleasure—wingtip tracks around the horizon.

Recovering carefully, nibbling the gentle buffet, the inverted horizon disappears down the windscreen. Vertically plunging, rolling slowly, I accelerate rapidly through 300 miles per hour. I aim for a larger patch of green and ease to the horizontal and power through this canyon in the clouds.

My senses ring. In a swift head movement, I pick up an incoming bogey, dark gray and closing fast. I turn hard—for a merge with my own shadow. Top slice the baby cumulus and imagine the phantom was a Focke Wolfe. I picture an alert youth diving in and out of cover, pulling firmly to break my lead, grunting whilst rotating his heavy head, searching for a clear tail with half an eye on his foe, snatching brief instrument scans. I have gone for height, staring back, waiting to reverse and take him out in a slashing dive. It is difficult to imagine the adrenaline. Experience the clammy sweat, the life or death fear of failure; the closing field of vision, feet and hands heavy under G, groping for combat flap, ranging the gun-sight with altimeter fast unwinding . . .

Back to reality. It's Sunday and my only opposition is fuel consumption and a planned airborne rendezvous with photographer John "Dibbsy" Dibbs.

On the Duxford channel a garbled call for take-off later changes to the discrete frequency. I estimate his breakout point and bushwhack the jet trainer as it climbs to the meeting point. I reverse the Mustang and slide carefully into echelon starboard and spy Dibbsy close up—all grins, arms, and lenses. After a few gentle turns, we hand signal for the formation vertical, as briefed. How does he hold that camera steady under G? I feel airspeed slacking now and the cameraship floats over the top. Gravity assists thrust as we accelerate toward the deck and slide into a series of steep wing overs. Sortie ended, we sweep down Duxford's turf for a run and break to land—jet for the hard, Mustang for the grass.

Pull hard and up, into the downwind, speed decaying rapidly through 160 miles per hour, 20 degrees of flap, gear-handle in the down detent—three greens. A curving base leg to short finals, full flap and 100 miles per hour over the hedge; prop to full fine and into peripheral vision as the nose comes up and the airfield disappears. Throttle closed, a short flare and stall as the mains and tail wheel kiss the grass. With a comic foot dance, stick full back and some light braking, we slow to a safe walking pace. Boost pumps off, mixture lean, oil-cooler and radiator doors open in manual, pressures and temperatures good at idle, flaps up. I slide open the side window and weave carefully back to dispersal.

Shut down checks complete, canopy open, helmet off. I feel the breeze. I taste the satisfaction. I stretch out on the now-dry Duxford grass, look back with complicity at the Mustang, contemplate my incredible privilege, and consider the responsibility. Imagine doing that for real 60 years ago.

—Stephen Grey, April 2002

THE GROUPS,
THE MACHINES,
THE ACES.

CHAPTER I

4TH FIGHTER GROUP – "The Debden Eagles"

334th, 335th, and 336th Fighter Squadrons

This famous Fighter Group in the 8th Air Force (AF) was activated on September 12, 1942, by the transfer to the USAAF of three RAF squadrons—Nos. 71, 121, and 133. Better known as the Eagle Squadrons, these legendary units were manned principally by U.S. volunteer pilots with RAF training and combat experience.

Nearly 250 U.S. pilots—none of whom had previously been in the USAAF (United States Army Air Force)—passed through the Eagle Squadrons. During their existence, the Eagles destroyed 73 German aircraft, but this success came at a high price—the lives of 77 U.S. and five RAF pilots.

The newly formed 4th Fighter Group (FG) was based at former RAF Debden, not far from Duxford, and remained there until after VE-Day. Its initial mount was the beloved Spitfire V, but on March 10, 1943, it received Republic P-47C Thunderbolts, which were nicknamed "Jug" (short for Juggernaut). Despite increasing operational success, many pilots complained about flying this huge aircraft after the sprightly Spitfire. The most vociferous was Commanding Officer (CO) Col. Don Blakeslee who called the P-47s "seven-ton monsters" and campaigned to have them replaced by P-51B Mustangs, which duly occurred on February 25, 1944. The Group operated the B-model until delivery of the classic P-51D in June 1944, and the P-51K in December 1944.

The 4th FG was the first in the newly formed 8th Air Force and the most successful in terms of claims—583 air victories and 468 enemy aircraft destroyed on the ground. In return, the 4th FG lost 241 aircraft in action.

Above: The 4th Fighter Group's legendary leader, Don Blakeslee, sitting in his Eagle Squadron Spitfire Mk V.

Right: Standing in front of Lt. John Godfrey's P-51B, *Reggie's Reply*, the pilots of the 4th FG illustrate combat tactics for the folks back home.

4TH FIGHTER GROUP – "The Debden Eagles"

Already an experienced private pilot, Don Blakeslee obtained an honorable discharge from the U.S. Army reserves in September 1940 in order to volunteer, at 22 years of age, for war service with the Royal Canadian Air Force.

After training in Ontario, Blakeslee was shipped to England in May 1941, and by the fall of that year, was flying Spitfire V combat missions with 401 Squadron RCAF. By the end of the year he had one confirmed victory with three other German fighters damaged. During the first five months of 1942, he claimed two FW190s destroyed and another damaged. He was then transferred to the newly formed RAF No. 133 (Eagle) Squadron, composed principally of American volunteers. His most successful sortie with that unit came during a huge aerial battle over Dieppe, France, where he destroyed a Dornier 217, claimed an FW190 probable, and damaged two 190s. Blakeslee's natural leadership saw him promoted to Squadron Leader, but he was soon busted back to Flight Lieutenant when caught with two WAAFs in his quarters!

When the Eagle Squadrons and their revered Spitfires Vs were transferred to the USAAF in September 1942, Blakeslee's experience was quickly recognized and he became a Major and CO of the 335th Fighter Squadron (FS). In March 1943, the squadron was issued the P-47 Thunderbolt, and despite his disparaging comments on the 47, Blakeslee soon scored his fifth victory and became an ace.

Shortly afterwards, in recognition of his outstanding leadership qualities, he

was promoted to Lieutenant Colonel and was appointed as the 4th FG Executive Officer. In December 1943, he was invited to lead the Mustang-equipped 354th FG on its first combat mission. He flew six missions with that group and downed an Me110.

His association with the 4th FG was soon regained when he was recalled as CO of the unit in January 1944. He quickly established his presence, and by the following month, he had succeeded and replaced the P-47s with the Mustang. Success was immediate and the group claimed a record-breaking 323 enemy aircraft within the first two months of P-51 operations. Blakeslee's participation in that score was 6.5 aerial victories and two ground kills.

In subsequent flights, ranging throughout Europe during the latter stages of the war, he completed his wartime total score of 15.5 aerial victories. Furloughed to the states in September 1944, he managed again to be posted as Commander of the 4th FG at Debden. However, after the capture of another famous and experienced commander, Hub Zemke, Blakeslee was deemed too valuable to risk in combat and was grounded by the 8th AFheadquarters.

Despite this setback, by the end of World War II, Blakeslee had flown more combat hours than any other U.S. fighter pilot and had inspired the 4th FG to become the highest scoring Group in the 8th AF. Leadership by example and teamwork were his skills and, in modesty, he never carried personal embellishments, decorations, or victory markings on his aircraft.

AAF. SPEC. PROJ. NO. 927779-R
U.S. ARMY P-51 D-20-NA
SERIAL NO. AAF 44-72339
CREW WEIGHT 200 LBS.

SERVICE THIS AIRPLANE WITH
GRADE 100/130 FUEL. IF NOT
AVAILABLE TO 90-3-1 WILL BE
CONSULTED FOR EMERGENCY ACTION
SUITABLE FOR AROMATIC FUEL.

WD

August 17, 1944. In an OP 519, Capt. Van Wyck led a Penetration Target Withdrawal Support to Les Foulens, France, from 0820 to 1415. Weather made the "sightseeing cruise'" uneventful for the Forts and Fighters.

Col. Blakeslee had to go out and get a new log book, no doubt to continue doctoring it in order to hide his total amount of combat time. Various estimates at the time were 1,300 hours. When Blakeslee was asked when he was going to quit, he said, "Hell, I'm just learning to fly!"

—4th Fighter Group OPs Log, Debden, 1944.

Above: Col. Blakeslee leads a tight three-ship over a typical English cloud bank.

Left: Col. Blakeslee (right) with some of the 4th's legendary aces in front of the group's scoreboard.

Right: First Russian Shuttle Mission to Pyratin. June 21, 1944

"Colonel Blakeslee's navigation was faultless and at exactly the briefed minute, the red-nosed ships of the 4th Group and our own blue-nosed planes swung over the bombers and began weaving out to the side and over the glistening B-17s. They had effectively bombed their target, Ruhland, and had reformed in two compact boxes. There is something dignified and majestic about a large formation of bombers plodding through the sky, and knowing we were flying over territory never before visited by American aircraft, a certain pride was felt by all. At the waist guns in some of those Big Friends, our crew chiefs were keeping a nervous eye peeled for the enemy. We didn't intend to let the enemy get a crack at our crew chiefs."

—Lt. Donald McKibben, 352nd FG. First Russian Shuttle Mission to Pyratin. June 21, 1944.

CAPT. DOMINIC "DON" GENTILE

4TH FIGHTER GROUP – "The Debden Eagles"

Ohio-born of Italian descent, Dominic Gentile tried to join the USAAC in 1941 but was turned down, perhaps because of his 300 hours of experience in sport planes. The RCAF enlisted him in August of 1941, and by December of that year he was on his way to England as a Pilot Officer. After further operational training, he was posted to the RAF's No. 133 Eagle Squadron that was composed principally of American volunteers and flying Spitfire Vs. His first combat mission was in June 1942, and his initial victories were in August of that year during the huge air battles over Dieppe, France. He shot down an FW190 plus a Ju-88 and was awarded the British Distinguished Flying Cross (DFC).

With the United States' entry into the war, the three RAF Eagle Squadrons were transferred to the USAAF and Gentile became a 2nd Lieutenant with the 336th FS of the 4th FG.

Although already an ace with six victories, Gentile was to become famous in a very short period for his exploits with the P-51B Mustang, which his crew decorated as *ShangriLa*. In March 1944, on an escort duty near Wittenburg, Germany, the squadron encountered 60-plus enemy fighters and Gentile downed two FW190s and damaged a Dornier 217, to open his series of rapid successes with the Mustang.

Within five days he paired with John Godfrey over Berlin to fend off a swarm of *Luftwaffe* fighters attacking B-17s. In their first bounce, Gentile and Godfrey each claimed an Me109. Within seconds Gentile disposed of a third and the pair

then flamed up a flight of two 109s but, as that was happening, Godfrey was attacked from the rear by another Messerschmitt. Gentile's official report read, "We turned into him and got him between us. I fired first and got strikes but overshot and told Lt. Godfrey to take over. He got strikes but ran out of ammo. I told him to cover me while I finished off the 109. Its belly tank caught fire and the German went down to 1,000 feet and bailed out."

On March 18, 1944, Gentile downed an FW190 near Augsburg, Germany, and five days later near Munster, Gentile again led Godfrey and nailed two 109s; his wingman got another. On March 27, near Cazaux in France, he destroyed two Me410s, and on the 29th of that month, he got three kills to bring his score to 19.8.

The newspapers started to talk of a race to beat the all-time score of 26 American victories held by Eddie Rickenbacker in World War I. On April 1, 1944, Gentile scored again, which, together with five aircraft destroyed in a strafing attack on Stendal Airfield, brought him closer to the title. On April 8, he entered the history books with three more downed aircraft. Recognition came on April 11, when General Eisenhower traveled to Debden and presented the Distinguished Service Cross (D.S.C.) to Gentile and the 4th FG Commander Don Blakeslee.

Gentile's last operational mission was on April 23, 1944. Newspaper reporters and photographers were present and had been promised a "buzz job" on his return, but unfortunately he got too low, and cracked up the Mustang. Thankfully, his pride was the only thing injured.

"I once passed the hut that housed the Catholic Chapel on my way to briefing and met Don Gentile coming out. 'What were you doing in there, Don?' he asked. 'Praying,' I said. 'I go there before every mission.' 'What do you pray for?' he asked. 'To shoot down more planes, of course!' I said. 'This time I prayed for three!'"

–Maj. Jim Goodson, 14-kill ace of the 336th FS/4th FG

LT. COL. CLAIREBORNE H. "ZOOT" KINNARD, JR.

4TH FIGHTER GROUP – "The Debden Eagles"

Zoot Kinnard became one of the few pilots to lead two 8th Air Force Groups—the 355th and the 4th. He received fighter training on the P-40 and P-47, which led to his first combat missions with the "Thud." He quickly demonstrated exceptional leadership qualities and it was not long before he was promoted to command the 354th FS of the 355th FG, based at Steeple Morden, England, in November 1943.

Because of a severe ear infection that permanently damaged his hearing, he was unable to fly with the 355th FG until February 1944, when he led a bomber escort mission to Frankfurt. Zoot had his first real contact with the enemy on March 29, when he led his squadron into a gaggle of more than 50 FW190s attacking B-17 Flying Fortresses over Brunswick. Although Kinnard didn't personally score, the squadron claimed 14 destroyed. Kinnard's time soon arrived, and on April 13, he took top honors of the day with one aerial victory and four destroyed on the ground while they swept *Luftwaffe* airdromes in the Munich area.

Missions over Holland, Belgium, France, Poland, and Germany followed until D-Day on June 6, 1944, and by that time the squadron had switched to the P-51B Mustang. Kinnard's was marked *Man-o'-War* with "The Bulldogs" (the squadron's adopted name) on the righthand cowling. On the day of the Normandy landings, Kinnard's role was to the south, and he operated as fighter/bombers attacked

road/rail transport in the Le Mans area. Operational records comment "Several ships came back with pieces of exploded trucks, railcars, and armored cars stuck in various locations on the bottom of their birds."

Kinnard was promoted to Group Executive Officer on June 8, 1944, and four days later he received a brand new P-51D with which he led the 354th FS to France on a B-24 escort mission. The 24th of June was a big day. Kinnard led the group to attack Angers, France, where he bagged 3 out of 24 enemy aircraft destroyed on the airfield. Early in July, the action reverted back to Germany and Kinnard broke up a mixed formation of German fighters attacking B-24s near Leipzig. He personally downed two Me410s and an Me109 to become an ace and received a D.S.C. for this action.

Zoot was transferred to the 4th FG towards the end of August 1944, first as No. 2, and then to become CO in early November. During that short time period, he downed two more Me109s and destroyed three more aircraft on the ground. After some well-earned leave in the United States, Kinnard was transferred back to the 355th FG as CO on February 21, 1945, and carried out a series of largely uneventful ramrod missions until they attacked Leck airfield and destroyed 12 new He111s, and Kinnard claimed 2.5. On April 10, he claimed two Me109s over Prague to finalize his war career with eight air and 17 ground victories.

"I saw a 109 coming toward me at 500 feet. I pulled up and fired at him from about 20 degrees coming head on—got hits in the engine, cockpit and left wing. I had to hit the deck immediately as the field defenses opened up. As I went over a little hill about 1,000 yards away, I looked back and saw that he had crashed and was burning."

—Lt. Col. Kinnard's encounter report for September 11, 1944. He was credited with a downed Bf109, for a total of six kills. This was his sole kill with the 4th FG.

CAPT. DONALD R. EMERSON

4TH FIGHTER GROUP – "The Debden Eagles"

Donald Emerson was born to a farm family in Joliette, North Dakota. He was 19 when America entered the hostilities and he volunteered for the U.S. Army Air Corps. While he finished training as an armorer, the age and educational requirements for pilot cadets were lowered and his application was accepted. By the end of 1943, he had received his wings and completed combat training on the Mustang. He commented, "It has a little sign in the cockpit that says 'Do not exceed airspeed of 500 miles per hour.' Hot Dog."

Emerson sailed to England in January 1944, for assignment to the P-51B-equipped 336th FS, a member of the already illustrious 4th FG led by Col. Don Blakeslee.

The razorback Mustang was quickly replaced by a bubble canopy P-51D and personalized with a combative Donald Duck decoration. In over 80 combat missions during his eight months in England, Emerson participated in the Russian Shuttle to Pyratin and on to Italy, as well as the D-Day operations.

On Christmas Day 1944, while the squadron provided support during the Battle of the Bulge over the Ardennes, he was set upon by six *Luftwaffe* FW190 fighters. He managed to shoot down two and elude the rest in a dense cloud cover. However, when he broke out at low-level, his Mustang was caught by anti-aircraft fire and he crashed into a British-occupied part of Belgium. He is thought to have died of wounds prior to impact. He was only 21 years old.

"I saw an FW190 with a silver Mustang behind him, which I cut off in a starboard turn. I was just ready to start pulling deflection on the enemy fighter when, to my amazement, the FW190 rolled over and the pilot bailed out. His chute opened immediately. The impression I got was that the pilot, seeing two Mustangs after him, decided to get out while the going was good."

—Lt. Emerson's encounter report for June 20, 1944. He was credited with an FW190 destroyed, which was his third victory.

Left: Flying close escort, Donald Emerson ensures a B-17's safe return, 1944.

"I was leading Becky Blue Section when two bogies passed under us from nine o'clock. As soon as we determined that they were bandits, we turned hard to starboard and opened up. The Me 410s headed for the bombers. Col. Blakeslee's section chased them line astern. They turned starboard, and my section dropped tanks and cut them off. One of the 410s split-S'd for the deck, and I continued after the other one. I closed rapidly taking several deflection shots and then closed line astern. I got several strikes which set his starboard engine on fire. I then pulled up to one side expecting him to explode or go into the deck as he was in a steep spiral. At that time, Lt. Netting had also made a pass at the 410 before I set it on fire. We formed-up and made a pass on several Seaplanes on a lake, but I only had one gun operating. I don't think I did much damage to the Do-18. I claimed one Me410 destroyed, shared with Lt. Netting, and one Do-18 damaged."

—Donald R. Emerson 1st Lt., AC. Combat Report, May 29, 1944

Right: Many fighter pilots were superstitious and depended on many things to get them through the war. Donald Emerson found comfort in his lucky rabbit foot.

MAJ. GERALD E. "MONTY" MONTGOMERY

4TH FIGHTER GROUP – "The Debden Eagles"

Born on July 10, 1922, Monty was raised in West Texas. On his 18th birthday, he made his way to Windsor, Canada, where he enlisted in the Royal Canadian Air Force. He received his wings in March 1942.

When he was old enough to qualify for the United States Army Air Corps, he initiated a transfer. While he waited for the transfer, he was assigned to Ottawa as a flight instructor where he met the British Prime Minister, Winston Churchill. Still in the RCAF, he was shipped to the U.K. where he flew Hurricanes. In February 1943, he was released by the RCAF and accepted into the U.S. Army Air Corps 6th Fighter Wing. He flew Spitfire Vs, followed by the P-47 Thunderbolt. On May 17, 1943, he joined the 334th Fighter Squadron, stationed at Debden in England.

Montgomery destroyed his first enemy aircraft, a Focke Wulf 190, on January 14, 1944, on a mission over France. Upon confirmation, he noted, "number one, no longer a virgin." Shortly afterwards an Associated Press photo showed Monty and two fellow 4th FG pilots sharing a $120 pool they won by shooting down the unit's 50th German aircraft.

In November 1944, while escorting Liberators over Minden, Germany, Monty got on the tail of a Messerschmitt and began to fire. The German passed over an airdrome, circled fast, lowered his wheels, made a hurried landing, and immediately taxied into the protection of a concrete hanger. Monty remarked, "the Hun scurried in like a rat going home to his hole." A week later, the squadron attacked 44 Me261s at an airdrome in Leipheim, Germany. As Monty and the others dove and strafed, he pulled out of the smoke and confronted another squadron plane. "We passed so close that I could hear his propeller." That should have told him he was using up his luck. He made yet another pass at 50 feet off the deck and was hit by a burst of flak. The stick went loose, but he made it back to base in England where they saw that the flak had carried away half of his tail surface.

Montgomery stayed with the 4th FG until the end of the war and was credited with 17.5 destroyed air and ground kills. He flew four different Mustangs, all marked *Sizzlin' Liz*.

Above: Monty Montgomery (center) shares the $120 "lucky pot" for his part in claiming the group's 50th victory, a FW 190, on January 14, 1944.

"The next plane in the line up was a Ju88. I fired one good burst at it and then sprayed several other planes parked further along the line. On the second pass across the field I saw that the Ju88 was afire. White smoke was pouring from the engines and the port wing was blazing."

—Capt. Montgomery's encounter report for March 27, 1944. He claimed three strafing kills on this day, and his final wartime tally for ground kills was 14.5, which made him one of the most successful strafing aces in the 4th FG.

Above: The stress of combat shows in this study of Montgomery shutting down *Sizzlin' Liz* after a lengthy escort mission.

"I picked out a Me109 that was in a slight turn ahead of me. I gave him one short deflection burst and he immediately pulled the nose straight up in a stalled condition. I put the bead just above the nose and gave him three seconds of fire. When I looked back the enemy aircraft was spinning. The Hun pulled out of the spin at 2,000 feet, but bailed out before I could get the nose up for another attack."

—Maj. Montgomery's encounter report for September 11, 1944.

Above: *Sizzlin' Liz* **in a revetment during the winter of 1944**

MAJ. PIERCE "MAC" MCKENNON

4TH FIGHTER GROUP – "The Debden Eagles"

Mac was born in Fort Smith, Arkansas, to an eminent medical practitioner and his musician wife. McKennon demonstrated a rare musical talent and won a university music scholarship. Studies did not last too long after Mac told his professor to file Debussy's works in a suitable recess, and then went to play with a boogie-woogie band.

Mac joined USAAC flight training in 1941, but flunked for "an inherent lack of flying ability," so he went to Canada to volunteer for the RCAF. By June 1942 he had completed training and was assigned to a reserve RCAF Spitfire squadron in the U.K.

It was February 1943 before he saw any combat, and it was as a 2nd Lieutenant in the USAAF with the 335th FS of the 4th FG at Debden, just as it transitioned from Spitfire Vs to P-47 Thunderbolts. Mac was memorable for eating every leftover of the pre-mission bacon and egg breakfast, and then sitting down at the mess piano singing "For Those About to Die," followed by the most outrageous boogie-woogie versions of "The Old Rugged Cross." By the time he was through with his performance, the pilots had lost their pre-combat jitters and were raring to go.

McKennon flew his first combat missions in a Spitfire V, but received his first aerial victory in a P-47 in July 1943. By the time of re-equipment with the P-51 Mustang in February 1944, he had four FW190s to his credit. With the P-51 he racked up success after success before he took a 20mm cannon round through the canopy and received wounds to his face. At 10.5 aerial victories by May 1944, he took leave stateside, and returned in August to his group in England as a Major and CO of the 335th FS.

Only 10 days into the job, his luck ran out during a strafing mission in France when his aircraft was one of five Mustangs shot down. Three of the pilots were killed and one was captured; McKennon managed to evade the enemy for nearly a month, and finally returned to Debden with the help of the French Maquis.

McKennon's final aerial victory came on Christmas Day during a major engagement over Bonn when he shared an Me109. Aerial resistance was scarce in early 1945, but the group started to systematically attack ground targets. On March 18, on escort over Berlin, he led part of the Group down over the Neubrandenburg airfield. He was hit by flak, and jumped shortly afterward. Lt. George Green of the 335th FS would not leave the "Boss" in Germany and bravely landed his Mustang alongside Mac. While the rest of the Mustangs provided fire cover, he threw his parachute away, and with Mac on his lap, took off and made a perfect landing back at Debden.

Not deterred by being shot down twice behind enemy lines, McKennon made many further strafing missions, and during the last full month of the war, achieved six more ground victories. As a tribute to his Arkansas ancestry, McKennon's Mustangs were decorated as *Ridge Runner* with a symbolic wild boar.

Above: Maj. "Mac" McKennon power-checks the Merlin on *Ridge Runner*.

"Our warmest memories of Debden were those precious evenings—each one of which could have been our last—with Mac McKennon. A cigarette dangling from his lower lip, pounding away till the beer in his mug perched on the piano was slopping over the top. Mac could transpose any melody into a rolling, rumbling boogie-woogie. He could always transform gloom, fear, and grief into relaxation, happiness, and hope."

—Maj. Jim Goodson, 14-kill ace of the 336 FS, 4th FG.

Above: At the Officer's Club in Debden, Mac treats the boys to some boogie-woogie.

CHAPTER 2

31ST FIGHTER GROUP – "Return with Honor"

307th, 308th, and 309th Fighter Squadrons

The 31st Pursuit Group (PG) was formed in February 1940 at Selfridge Field, Michigan, and was initially comprised of the 39th, 40th, and 41st Pursuit Squadrons (PS). In January 1942 they were replaced by the 307th, 308th, and 309th Squadrons equipped with Curtiss P-40B Tomahawks and Bell P-39 Airacobras.

The group shipped out to England in June 1942 and was re-equipped with the Spitfire Vb. Under RAF control and operating from RAF bases Atcham, High Ercall, and temporarily, Biggin Hill, Kenley, and Westhampnett, the Group fought in the Dieppe raids and sweeps from Le Havre to Abbeville and Calais. By September 14, the group was transferred from the 8th Air Force to the 12th, which was dedicated to the Mediterranean Theater of Operations.

In keeping with its somewhat nomadic existence, October 23, 1942, saw the 31st FG on ships to Gibraltar, from where it commenced a North African campaign fighting the Vichy French, *Luftwaffe,* and Italian air forces from bases in Algeria, Tunisia, and Morocco. By May 1943, the Germans in North Africa had surrendered and the group was re-equipped with the Spitfire IX and VIII in time for the push north into Pantellaria, Gozo, and Sicily. From bases in Sicily and Southern Italy,

the Group supported the Salerno and Anzio landings with ground attack, point defense, and bomber escort missions.

Between August 1942 and March 1944, the 31st FG and its Spitfires had destroyed 194 enemy aircraft. Thereafter, it was transferred to the 15th Strategic Air Force and re-equipped with P-51B Mustangs, which were ferried from North Africa to bases in newly liberated Eastern Italy. From San Severo, the Group principally carried out bomber escort duties that ranged widely to Romania, Hungary, Austria, Southern Germany, and France. In July 1944, it participated in the 'Frantic III' operations and flew onwards from their Romanian targets to Pyratin in Ukraine where it hit airfields in Poland. On the Group's return to Italy, it received a Presidential Unit Citation for 82 enemy aircraft downed in the month of July.

Re-equipped with the P-51D, the group supported the landings in Southern France and carried out bomber escort missions to Czechoslovakia, Yugoslavia, Austria, Romania, Hungary, and Germany; and Berlin finally became a target from Italy.

The 31st FG ended the war as top-scoring Allied Fighter Group in the Mediterranean Theater of Operations and the fifth highest overall, with 570 aerial victories.

Right: The 31st Fighter Group pictured at its airfield in San Severo, Italy, in 1944.

Crew Chief SSgt. Carpenter
Armorer Cpl. Langlois
SPECIAL PROJECT .30694-R
D-5 NA
44-13500

Lt. Goebel

31ST FIGHTER GROUP – "Return with Honor"

Born and raised in Ohio, John Voll volunteered for flight training in March 1943, and graduated in January 1944. He was shipped overseas in May to join the 308th FS, 31st FG with the 15th Strategic Air Force in Italy, and flew Mustangs.

From a very young rookie on his first combat mission in mid-May 1944, to his final amazing victories in mid-November 1944, Voll displayed great courage, skill, and outstanding luck to become the top scoring ace in the Mediterranean Theater of Operations with 21 aerial victories, 2 probables, and 2 damaged in just six action-packed months.

Mounted in his personally decorated P-51D *American Beauty*, Voll and his squadron roamed far and wide over Italy, Austria, Yugoslavia, Romania, Czechoslovakia, Hungary, France, and Germany. His first victory was a FW190 over Ploesti, Romania. Further victories over Me109s and Me210s followed until he became an ace on July 2, when he

shot down a 109 from a swarm that attacked USAAF bombers over Budapest, Hungary.

His 13th victory could have been unlucky. As he closed on a vapor-trailing Macchi 202, he found another on his tail. As Voll noted, "My shots blew the cockpit apart and the pilot bailed out. I started to attack the other plane, but by this time another had joined the fight. Since the Macchi can turn a shade sharper than the Mustang, they soon had me boxed. I got into a cloud and headed for home."

In November 1944, Voll was returning from a mission to Germany when he sighted a Ju-88 over Northern Italy. While in the 'bounce,' seven FW190s swept out of the sun and five Me109s joined the party. Voll closed rapidly on the Ju-88 and destroyed it before he turned in to the 12 angry bandits. Before the fight was over he had downed two 190s and a 109, and damaged several others. He characterized this encounter as, "actually, it was just a matter of shooting everything that passed in front of me."

"As the flaming Ju-88 fell to the sea below, Captain Voll looked up and his blood ran cold. Poised in a V-formation directly above him were 12 German fighters, seven FW190s, and five Me109s. At the very moment he saw them, they peeled off in a massed attack against the one, lone American Mustang with the red diagonal stripes on its tail. In a furious blur of wheeling, screaming wings, and engines, all straining for one extra square foot of lift or one horsepower beyond maximum to outdo the enemy and grant one of them the merest measure of advantage. Captain Voll did no less than destroy four of these enemy fighters, probably destroyed two more, and damaged another two. The four remaining fighters fled in terror at this marvel of a man and his machine, so perfectly, lethally matched."

—31st Fighter Group Daily War Diary entry for November 16, 1944.

Above: John Voll pictured in P-51D *American Beauty* during an escort mission.

"On our way home during a mission, I saw a Macchi 202 through a break in the clouds and went after him. Going in and out of the clouds, as we were, I was chasing his vapor trails rather than actually seeing him all the time, and when I finally got into position to fire I glanced back and there was another Macchi on my tail. I started firing, and although I only used up 20 rounds from each gun on the Macchi in front of me, it seemed as though I'd used a 100 before my shots blew the cockpit apart and the pilot bailed."

—Lt. Voll's encounter report for September 23, 1944. He was credited with a Macchi C202 destroyed, his 13th victory.

CAPT. ROBERT J. GOEBEL

31ST FIGHTER GROUP – "Return with Honor"

A Wisconsin born, all-American boy of German stock, Bob Goebel received his wings in 1943. He was initially posted to the Panama Canal zone on defensive duties, and flew the P-39K Airacobra with the 43rd FS.

At the turn of the year, he transferred to the 31st FG's 308th FS, which shipped to North Africa to join the 15th AF where the 20-year-old pilot received combat training on Spitfire Vs and Spitfire VIIIs. On completion of the training, the squadron was moved across the Mediterranean to a forward airfield at San Severo in newly Allied-occupied Southern Italy, just 20 miles from the enemy lines. Its role was changed to bomber escort and the group was re-equipped with the P-51B Mustang. Goebel noted, "Not the sweet feel of the beloved Spit … a different breed of airplane … set apart by its range."

After just 15 hours of Mustang training, Goebel's first combat mission was on April 16, 1944, when he escorted B-24s to targets in Romania, over the Adriatic Sea and the mountains of Western Yugoslavia. It was a "milk run" except for the loss of two P-51s to the gunners of the B-24s they were escorting!

His first air-to-air combat with Me109s was over Wiener Neustadt, Austria. Goebel related it as, "The dogfight was the damnedest melee I have ever been involved in. I wrenched my plane into a turn … the leader made a sudden violent reversal which the wingman failed to follow. A bad mistake. I was down to 350 yards. I opened fire, hosing away at nearly 30 degrees of deflection … rewarded with a few strikes on the forward fuselage. His [the leader's] canopy came off, followed instantly by a dark hurtling figure. I had prided myself in keeping pretty cool in the air. Now I babbled excitedly and disgracefully on the R/Tå, calling for my flight to witness my first victory."

In 61 missions, the gallant Bob Goebel roamed over Romania, Germany, Austria, France, Hungary, Czechoslovakia, Yugoslavia, and Italy. He destroyed a total of 10 Me109s and one Me110, with an additional 109 probable—three Me109s of that total were taken out in one sortie. When he returned home after his extended tour of duty, he was a veteran at 21 years of age.

"Back in Wisconsin when I was a kid, Germans were often referred to as Dutchme. I knew the *Flying Dutchman* was a phantom ship, and so my P-51D was named."

"Compared with the P-39s, P-40s, and Spitfires that I had flown before, I soon found out that the Merlin-engined Mustang was indeed a different breed of airplane. It was fast, for one thing. The Mustang indicated 250 to 260 miles per hour at low altitude, compared with about 210 for the P-39 and the P-40 at cruise power. The P-51 was red lined at 505, and although it was no Spitfire, its turning ability wasn't bad at all—especially if you sneaked down 10 degrees of flaps. It was pretty good in the climbing department, too, and accelerated very fast in a dive. But the thing that really set the Mustang apart from any other fighter, friend or foe, was its range. With a 75-gallon tank slung under each wing, it could perform the unheard-of—it could fly six-hour missions."

—2nd Lt. Bob Goebel, 308th FS, 31st FG, 1944.

58

Crew Chief SSgt Carpenter   Lt. Goebel
Armorer Cpl. Langlois
AAF SPECIAL PROJECT NO. 90694-R
U.S. ARMY P-51B-5-NA
SERIAL NO. AAF 44-13500

Flying DUTCHMAN

CHAPTER 3

THE 78TH FIGHTER GROUP – "Above the Foe"

82nd, 83rd, and 84th Fighter Squadrons

The 78th Pursuit Group was activated in February 1942 in Indiana, and moved to Hamilton, California, between May and November 1942 for training on the Lockheed P-38 Lightning. The Group was shipped out to England via the luxury liner *Queen Elizabeth* with 13,000 other passengers. Its personnel arrived at Goxhill, Lincolnshire, in December 1942 to join the 8th Air Force. In February 1943, most of the pilots and P-38Gs were transferred to the 12th Air Force in support of Operation Torch, the North African landings.

The 78th found itself reformed within the 8th AF, re-equipped, and trained with the first operational Republic P-47C Thunderbolts. The Group was first based from Goxhill, but then was transferred in April 1943 to the famous RAF base at Duxford, Cambridgeshire, where it remained until the cessation of hostilities. Duxford, a permanent RAF base built by German prisoners during World War I, became affectionately known as the Duckpond.

The Group operated the P-47C on "Rodeo" sweeps and bomber escort duties to France, Belgium, and Holland until June 1943 when it received P-47Ds equipped with belly tanks. These aircraft enabled the bombers to be escorted into the heart of Germany and back. The Group first painted its trademark black-and-white checker-

board noses in April 1944, followed by D-Day recognition stripes in June 1944. Allied Fighter Command labeled the first day missions of the European Invasion "Full House," "Stud," and "Royal Flush," perhaps in recognition of the enormous gamble being taken. The group carried out "Rhubarb'" strafing and bombing missions behind the beachheads with great success.

Flak suppression and air support duties for Market Garden, the Allied airborne assault at Arnhem, were extremely difficult for the Group, which suffered 18 losses in 20 missions. Thereafter, it principally continued with bomber escort missions until December 1944, when it was re-equipped with the P-51D.

This aircraft enabled a wider range of operations, including escorts deep into Germany and flying onward to Poltava in Russia. Toward the end of the war as the *Luftwaffe* ran out of fuel, the escort missions also turned into gigantic airfield strafing exercises all over Germany and into occupied Czechoslovakia.

From its first combat operation in April 1943, until the last in April 1945, the 78th FG flew a total of 450 missions, 80,000 operational hours, and claimed 326 enemy aircraft destroyed, 25 probables, and 123 damaged as well as 362 destroyed on the ground. In the process, the group lost 167 aircraft in action with 97 pilots killed. It was the only 8th AF Group to have flown the P-38, P-47, and P-51.

Right: *Big Beautiful Doll*, Duxford, 1945.

COL. JOHN D. LANDERS

THE 78TH FIGHTER GROUP – "Above the Foe"

John Landers was commissioned as a Second Lieutenant and received his wings in December 1941. Thereafter, he served with the 9th FS of the 49th Pursuit Group in the Pacific Theater and flew P-40s.

He completed six aerial victories against the Japanese before he was shot down during December 1942. Landers evaded capture, returned to American battle lines, and was subsequently posted to the United States for a stint as a flight instructor.

Anxious to return to combat status, he was finally sent to the 38th FS of the 55th FG based at Nuthampstead in Hertfordshire, England. The Group flew the large Lockheed P-38 Lightnings and had suffered losses due to the aircraft's poor high altitude performance and susceptibility to engine failures at low temperatures. The pilots also suffered from extreme cockpit discomfort as a result of poor heating. The Lightning's role as escort fighter was reduced and the unit was more frequently used to attack airfields in France and the Low Countries. Landers became CO of the 38th FS in mid-1944 and was heavily involved in "Chattanooga" missions against rail transport, and "Jackpots" against airfields until the time of the D-Day assault landings. In that time period, the Group moved to a base at Wormingford, Essex. During a mission to the Halle area of the Third Reich, Landers led an attack on Me410s that pursued Liberators, shot down three, and damaged four.

In July 1944, the group traded in its P-38s for P-51D Mustangs, and in October of that year, Landers became Group Executive Officer of the 357th FG and raised his score to 11 victories in the first of the Mustangs painted as *Big Beautiful Doll*. In December he was promoted to Command the 78th FG at Duxford. He became

famous for his nose-low, two-point landings and his colorful black-and-white checkerboard version of *Big Beautiful Doll* with which he raised his overall score to 14.5.

Above: Col. Landers "mans up" for a mission in 1945.

"The P-51 was the best all-round fighter I flew in the war. It could do everything well, at high or low altitudes, and at the longest ranges of any fighter of World War II. Its Merlin engine was vulnerable to ground fire, but I was able to score 17 strafing victories in two missions in April 1945."

—Lt. Col. John D. Landers

"When we arrived, at least 80 planes were scattered around the field. When we left, there were 80 funeral pyres. A dozen anti-aircraft gunners put up some light flak at first, but it didn't bother us much, and we simply set up a traffic pattern. German aircraft were blowing up and burning all over the place. We made eight to nine passes. I scored doubles on each of my first three passes, two of the six planes blowing up."

–Lt. Col. Landers' encounter report for April 16, 1945. The 78th FG destroyed no fewer than 125 aircraft on the ground on this day, and 9 of them were credited to Landers.

Above: *The Big Beautiful Doll* looking resplendent in its revetment at Duxford, summer 1945.

"I charged my guns and came back into the fight. Four of my '50s' fired, and as I turned with an enemy aircraft, two of them stopped firing. The German pilot had had enough though. He bailed out. I quickly lined up on another 109, fired a short burst, and all my guns quit once more. Again this was a sufficient scare for the inexperienced German pilot who went over the side. All my kills on this mission were freaks. The Jerry pilots were very inexperienced, and all still played follow the leader."

—Col. John D. Landers' encounter report for March 2, 1945. Both of the destroyed Bf109s were from JG301.

CHAPTER 4

339TH FIGHTER GROUP – "Fowlmere Strafers"

503rd, 504th, and 505th Fighter Squadrons

The 339th FG was activated in February 1943 and worked up to combat status with the P-39 Airacobra. Its first combat mission was flown in P-51Bs on April 30, 1944, from Fowlmere, near Cambridge, England. The former home of No 19 Sqn RAF, flew Spitfires through the Battle of Britian. Fowlmere was a satellite airfield to the nearby Duxford, home of the 78th Fighter Group.

The Group soon changed to P-51Ds, and despite starting late, made its mark when it destroyed the most enemy aircraft on the ground (609) in its first year of combat operations. As "strafers extraordinary," the 339th's squadrons were the first to destroy 100-plus enemy aircraft in a day (April 10, 1945). It repeated the exercise just a week later with 118 enemy aircraft destroyed on the ground. This was a period when the *Luftwaffe* was very short of gasoline to fly their aircraft due to strategic bombing of oil installations, refineries, and transport.

In the air, the Group had 233 confirmed kills, which when combined with a ground score of 423, made it one of the most efficient fighter units per mission in the 8th Air Force at the end of European conflict.

Above: Members of the 503rd FS are about to partake in some "R&R" gaming in the English fields surrounding Fowlmere.

Right: Lt. Owen P. Farmer, pilot of 339th FG Mustang, "Dibbo," and his ground crew at Fowlmere in June 1944. Note the hasty application of invasion stripes.

LT. ROBERT "BOB" J. FRISCH

339TH FIGHTER GROUP – "Fowlmere Strafers"

The combat experience of Lt. Robert "Bob" J. Frisch was typical of many of the Mustang pilots that patrolled the skies over Europe during the latter stages of the war. He finished his training in Florida on the P-40 as the D-Day invasion took place in Europe. He was sent to England in September 1944, and joined the 503rd FS of the 339th FG based at Fowlmere, near Duxford in Cambridgeshire.

Issued with P-51D serial 44-14118, squadron-coded D7-J, Frisch named the aircraft *Worry Bird* after a mascot his girlfriend had sent him that he kept in the cockpit.

Aside from bomber escort missions flown in the expansive frozen European skies of 1944, Frisch also flew many strafing operations during the Battle of the Bulge. The winter of 1944–1945 was particularly horrendous. Missions called for pre-dawn take-offs from PSP runways with as little as three oil burner flares to illuminate the path. A member of the ground crew with a torch waved them clear to roll as direct forward visibility was nil due to the Mustang's nose-high ground attitude.

"Strafing a target of opportunity was always dangerous. You couldn't fly across the field and just keep turning round and shooting the aircraft up. You would make one pass, at a hundred feet or less, as fast as the Mustang would let you go, hit something, and get out. Going back simply was not an option for the airfield gunners would be ready and waiting."

Frisch flew 61 missions in seven months to complete his tour with credits of six (ground) kills and one damaged (air) Me109.

"The adrenaline was the whole thing ... You didn't register much during a scrap. It hit you on the way home... or after... you know someone had died."

—Lt. Robert J. Frisch

"We were at 25,000 feet and the bombers we were escorting were at 23,000. Someone yelled 'bogies' and we dropped tanks and firewalled the throttle, my training served me well as I was able to hang on to Lt. Stillwell while he chose his target, despite it being only my third mission. Someone else called they were 109's as we closed. The ensuing dogfight saw 9 German fighters fall."

—Lt. Robert J. Frisch

Above: *Worry Bird* above England on a training sortie.

CHAPTER 5

352ND FIGHTER GROUP – "Blue-Nosed Bastards of Bodney"

328th, 486th, and 487th Fighter Squadrons

Constituted in the United States in 1942, the 352nd FG sailed on the *Queen Elizabeth* on July 1, 1943, and headed for Europe. The men gambled their way to England. Blackjack and poker was played night and day until "Lady Luck" elected the minority richer and the majority poorer.

By early July, the Group was installed at Bodney, a former RAF Fighter Command grass base between Norwich and Kings Lynn. It had hard parking stands in the woods surrounding the field, but initially no permanent mess hall or technical facilities were present.

The Group first flew the Republic P-47 Thunderbolt, the type of aircraft it had trained with in the United States. It was September 1943 before the Group carried out its first combat mission, a bomber escort to France. The German *Luftwaffe* did not take long to figure out the range limitations of the P-47 and held back its defending fighters until the bombers became unescorted on the way in and out of the targets.

The solution came in April 1944 when the Group commenced re-equipment with the P-51B. With drop tanks, the fighters could now roam far and wide over Germany. The 8th AF Command initially allocated the 352nd FG a blue nose-color

code, and covered the spinner and a 12-inch band behind the propeller. By the end of the month, the distinctive sweep back to the canopy became the norm, as did the appearance of personalized aircraft names. Legend has it that Goering baptized them the "Blue-Nosed Bastards of Bodney" when he saw the group flying over Berlin.

The 486th FS flew, along with squadrons from the 4th FG, the first Shuttle mission and escorted bombers from England to Germany and onwards to land in Russia. The mission then operated from Russia, then to Italy, and back to England.

By the end of hostilities, the Group had flown 420 combat missions, and destroyed 791 enemy aircraft; 504 were in the air. Twenty-seven of its pilots were aerial aces, and four became "aces in the day." Maj. George E. Preddy claimed six Me109s as aerial victories in one sortie. He went on to become the top scoring Mustang ace with 26 aerial victories. He was shot down and killed by friendly fire from the U.S. 12th Anti-Aircraft Group while he pursued *Luftwaffe* fighters on Christmas Day 1944. The other aces in the day were Capt. William T. Whisner, pilot of *Princess Elizabeth* and *Moonbeam McSwine*; Capt. Donald S. Bryan; and Lt. Carl J. Luksic. Twelve 352nd FG pilots scored victories over German jet fighters while flying P-51s.

Right: George Preddy and Bill Whisner, two of the top aces of the 352nd Fighter Group—and one of the most successful pairings of leader and wingman—pose for the press at Bodney in 1944.

LT. COL. JOHN C. MEYER

352ND FIGHTER GROUP – "Blue-Nosed Bastards of Bodney"

John Meyer dropped out of Dartmouth College and joined the USAAC in 1939, and received his wings and commission in July 1940. At first he was an instructor, and then flew P-40s with the 33rd Pursuit Group in Iceland. Subsequently, he joined the 352nd FG and flew P-47s in Massachusetts, before he shipped out to Bodney, England, in June 1943. By the spring of 1944, Meyer had three confirmed victories and one probable.

The advent of the P-51B put Meyer on the map. In April he increased his score to 10.5 and was promoted to Lieutenant Colonel. By May he had pushed his total up to 15.5 and was sent home on leave. He returned to Bodney in August 1944, as Commander of the 487th FS. On an early mission he was hit by flak over France and was lightly wounded in the thigh. Back in the saddle 12 days later, he started to rack up aerial and ground victories until he had raised his total to 25.5 by mid-September. In late November he added three more aerial kills in one mission and was awarded a second D.S.C.

December 1944 produced bad weather, the German Ardennes offensive, and a call for close air support of the Allied Armies. The 8th AF lent the 352nd and 361st FG to the 9th AF. Meyer arrived at a forward base, Y-29 Asch Belgium, on December 23. He downed 2.5 enemy aircraft on the 26th, and on the 27th, he downed two more. He finished up 1944 with the destruction of an Arado 234 German jet bomber near Bonn.

On New Years Day, 150 Allied planes were destroyed in a massive *Luftwaffe* attack on forward bases. However, Meyer had anticipated the possibility and banned any 'festivities' the night before. When the Germans came to hit Asch, Meyer led 12 Mustangs down the runway straight into the oncoming mass of FW190 and Me109s. He immediately downed a Focke Wulf and chased another to Liege before hedestroyed it. This brought his aerial victories to 24 with 13 strafing ground kills. The other 11 P-51 pilots claimed a further 21 victories for no losses. The action earned Meyer his third D.S.C., and the 487th FS received a Distinguished Unit Citation (D.U.C.).

Charlie Goodman, a ground observer, wrote, "The piloting skills of both Americans and Germans were being displayed under a 2,000 foot ceiling with broken scud clouds underneath, making it a game of hide and seek. Thundering explosions, plumes of black smoke climbing into the sky, as many as 10 marking the fallen aircraft around the perimeter of the field. Suddenly a P-47 from the 366th across the field roaring down the runway to do a victory roll-breaks off at the three-quarter point when he realizes he is in the middle of a battle. He and his men join the fray. Finally the Germans withdrew, two Spitfires going balls-out chasing them back east."

Unfortunately just after the fight, Meyer was badly injured in a road accident when an ammunition carrier overturned on snowy roads. It was an unfortunate early end to the European adventures of a great fighter pilot, who nevertheless retained his position as the 8th AF's leading ace.

"Maj. Meyer had just landed his P-51 after a victorious mission, and he told S/Sgt. Conkey (crew chief) and me to get the airplane ready for the next mission, and be sure to get those new swastikas painted on. Knowing the amount of work required to prepare the Mustang for its next mission, Sgt. Conkey's response was less than enthusiastic, and he stated the swastikas were a low priority to him. Meyer's comeback was swift and to the point. 'No Sgt. Conkey. In my book it ranks high and here's why. On one of my early missions two German fighters covered in victory markings flew alongside me and looked me over. Scared the hell out of me. Now that I have the opportunity to do the same, if I can't shoot them down, I'll scare them down.' Needless to say, we damn well painted those swastikas onto his airplane."

–T/Sgt. Bill Kohlhas, Lt. Col. Meyer's assistant crew chief. He helped maintain his Mustang when Meyer was CO of the 487th FS in 1944.

Right: The Mustang Lt. Col. Meyer flew before *Petie 3rd* was known as *Petie 2nd*. This aircraft was damaged in a ground handling accident, and the Colonel wasted no time and traded it in for a brand-new P-51. *Petie 2nd* was repaired and given to Lt. Sheldon Heyer who renamed it *Sweetie Face*.

MAJ. GEORGE E. PREDDY, JR.

352ND FIGHTER GROUP – "Blue-Nosed Bastards of Bodney"

George Preddy, from Greensboro, North Carolina, was of slight and short build. He made three attempts to engage as a Naval aviator in 1939, but despite being an experienced barnstormer pilot, he was turned down. Not one to take "no" for an answer, his persistence paid off when he was finally accepted into the Army Air Corps. By the time he had completed his training, America was at war and he was sent to Australia with the 9th Squadron, 49th Pursuit Group. There he flew the P-40 in combat and damaged two Japanese aircraft before he was seriously injured following an air-to-air collision with another Warhawk. Sadly the other pilot was killed.

Months later, Preddy was in the states and wanted another fighter assignment. He was recommended to his future commander, John C. Meyer. After an interview, Meyer turned to Preddy's sponsor, I.B. "Jack" Donalson, and said, "Are you sure we got the right guy ... this fellow could not punch his way out of a paper bag." Preddy was nevertheless hired and undertook training on the Thunderbolt at Westover, Mississippi.

They shipped out to Bodney, England on the liner *Queen Elizabeth* during the summer of 1943. His first success did not come until December 1943, when he downed an Me109. He got two more kills before he received a P-51B he named *Cripes a' Mighty II*. From mid-April, Preddy began to roll up the victories with four more kills and a shared kill. On June 12, 1944, he traded his aircraft for a P-51D, a Mustang he named *Cripes a' Mighty 3rd,* and this was the aircraft with which Preddy became famous.

It all began on June 20, when Preddy downed a FW190 and shared a Me410 over Magedeburg. Within just a month, on July 18, near Warnemunde, the squadron encountered 40-plus Me210s and Ju-88s covered by 20 Me109s. Leading his flight, Preddy flamed a 109, destroyed three Ju-88s, and damaged two others. On August 5, he racked up 2.5 more victories and one ground kill.

On August 6, his "big day," Preddy nursed a massive hangover as he lead the group as relief for Meyer. In the ensuing melee, Preddy claimed six confirmed victories in five minutes of battle. When he landed at Bodney after this extraordinary sortie, he commented, "I just kept shooting and they just kept falling ... never again." He was awarded the D.S.C. and left to visit his family.

Preddy returned to Bodney in late October and was nominated as CO of the 328th FS. The 2nd of November saw a big push when he escorted bombers to the Merseburg refinery. A huge force of enemy fighters met them. The 328th tore into a gaggle of 50-plus Me109s, and within 15 minutes, Preddy's team had downed 25 aircraft—a new 8th AF record for a squadron on a single sortie. Preddy scored one.

In December 1944, the group was transferred to the Y29 forward airfield at Asch, Belgium. On Christmas Day, Major Preddy was soon in the thick of it, knocked out two Me109s near Koblenz, and brought his score to 26.83 aerial victories. Vectored to Liege to intercept low flying bandits, he spotted a '190' on the deck and chased it through the tree tops into an area guarded by the U.S. 12th Anti-Aircraft unit. Hit by 0.50 calibers from a U.S. Quad, he chandelled up to 700 feet, and his canopy came off, but he was unable to parachute. Tragically, *Cripes a Mighty 3rd* and the top Mustang ace of World War II died from friendly fire.

Above: Maj. George E. Preddy signals "six in a day!"
Right: George Preddy atop *Cripes a' Mighty 3rd*, with 23 kill markings emblazoned along the nose.

CRIPES A'MIGHTY 3RD

CHIEF · S/Sgt LEW LUNN
ASST · Cpl RED McVAY
ARM · Sgt M.G. KUHANECK

"I opened fire on one near the rear of the formation from 300 yards dead astern and got many hits around the cockpit. The enemy aircraft went down inverted and in flames. At this time, Lt. Doleac became lost while shooting down an Me 109 that had gotten on Lt. Heyer's tail. Lt. Heyer and I continued our attack and I drove up behind another enemy aircraft getting hits around the wing roots and setting him on fire after a short burst. He went spinning down and the pilot bailed out at 20,000 feet. I then saw Lt. Heyer on my right shooting down another enemy aircraft. The enemy formations stayed together taking practically no evasive action and tried to get back for an attack on the bombers who were now off to the right. We continued with our attack on the rear end (of the enemy formation) and I fired another from close range. He went down smoking badly and I saw him begin to fall apart below us. At this time, four other P-51s came in to help us with the attack. I fired at another 109 causing him to burn after a short burst. He spiraled down to the right in flames. The formation headed down and in a left turn keeping themselves together in rather close formation. I got a good burst into another one causing him to burn and spin down. The enemy aircraft were down to 5,000 feet now and one pulled off to the left. I was all alone with them now so went after this single 109 before he could get on my tail. I got in an ineffective burst causing him to smoke a little. I pulled into a steep climb to the left above him and he climbed after me. I pulled in as tight as possible and climbed at about 150 miles per hour. The Hun opened fire on me but could not get enough deflection to do any damage. With my initial speed, I slightly out-climbed him. He fell off to the left and I dropped down astern of him. He jettisoned his canopy as I fired a short burst getting many hits. As I pulled past, the pilot bailed out at 7,000 feet. I had lost contact with all friendly and enemy aircraft so headed home alone."

—Maj. George E. Preddy, Combat Report, August 6, 1944. Six Me109s destroyed.

Above: Recorded upon the moment of his return from the legendary August 6th, 1944, sortie by an Air Force photographer, this candid study of George Preddy bears witness to the fatigue and strain many of these young men endured.

"They saw us coming and turned into us. I singled one out and he started down, turning and taking evasive action. He went into a thin cloud and I went below after him. He turned into me and I dropped 20 degrees of flaps, enabling me to out-turn him. He then went down right on the deck and tried to outrun me, but I closed in on him and began firing from 400 yards dead astern. I got hits on the fuselage and left wing and he began smoking. As I pulled up past him, he ran into the ground and blew up."

—Maj. George E. Preddy, Combat Report, July 21, 1944. One Me109 destroyed.

"I have yet to meet a man with such single-minded and dedicated purpose. With such intense desire to excel, not for himself, but for his squadron and for his country. Above all, always, for his country. His appearance and conduct on the ground belied his skill, tenacity, and fighting heart in the air, but his achievements confirmed them. George Preddy was the greatest fighter pilot who ever squinted through a gun sight. He was the complete fighter pilot."

—Gen. John C. Meyer, Commanding Officer, 352nd Fighter Group.

CAPT. WILLIAM T. WHISNER

352ND FIGHTER GROUP – "Blue-Nosed Bastards of Bodney"

Louisianan Bill Whisner first came into prominence as wingman to the famous ace George Preddy. In January 1944, he was there as protection when Preddy claimed his first victim. Whisner scored his first personal victory against a 109, while he covered Preddy's lead.

Whisner's combat character was evidenced by a sortie over Vechta *Luftwaffe* base on April 9. He had a fright when a canopy panel exploded during a high-speed dive. Thinking he had been hit, Whisner pulled up, assessed the damage, and dived down again to wreck two Ju-88s and a barracks with his accurate strafing. On the 20th, over Clermont-Ferrand in France, he had an aerial victory against a FW190; followed with another 190 on the 29th after a long scrap. For 15 minutes they twisted and turned from high altitude all the way down to the ground. The 190 looped off of the deck in an attempt to crash the Mustang. On the second tight loop, Wisner was able to get in a deflection shot and see his quarry dive straight into a forest.

The next day, Whisner was flying over Magdeburg as an element leader in Preddy's flight. Preddy ran out of ammo during a melee with a bunch of 109s and called on Whisner to finish off a smoker. This was Whisner's last victory until his return for a second tour in the Fall of 1944.

On November 2, 1944, Whisner was over Merseburg in his new P-51D, *Moonbeam McSwine*, when he nailed a 109 from a gaggle of 50-plus 109s that were attacking B-17s. The 352nd group racked up 38 kills that day. Whisner's

personal 'Big Day' was November 21, when he was again over the refineries at Merseburg, a target for more than 700 B-17s. Lt. Col. J. C. Meyer was leading a section with Whisner in charge of Green Flight when a huge gaggle of FW190s, at varying higher altitudes, attacked the rear of the bombers. Whisner clobbered one at 200 yards and then took major chunks out of another, which entered a flat spin into the haze. He attached himself to the enemy formation and nailed another from 100 yards. Pulling up, he crossed another 190, which flamed under a 20 degrees deflection shot. Like a bulldog, he returned to the enemy formation and downed another two 190s. The other Focke Wulfes dropped their belly tanks and three of them bounced Whisner, who shoved *Moonbeam*'s throttle to the wall and out-climbed them to 25,000 feet. He saw another 190 on the tail of a P-51 and dived too close at 50 yards to cut the 190 to bits with a hail of fire. Only five of the seven enemy aircraft were eventually confirmed. The second and fourth victories were rated a probable because it only had been filmed spinning into the haze, trailing smoke. Whisner received a D.S.C. for this courageous sortie. Two 109s then fell to Whisner's P-51D on the 27th.

On Christmas Eve, after they flew bomber cover to Germany, the "Blue-Nosers" landed back at Y29. In the early hours of the new year, the *Luftwaffe* attacked the base. Col. J. C. Meyer had premised that the Germans would attack, thinking that the "Amis" would be nursing headaches, and threw his squadron into the air as the *Luftwaffe* arrived. Whisner scored as he was still climbing.

(continued on pg 100)

Right: Capt. Whisner poses beside his P-51B, *Princess Elizabeth.*

"During the last six months of 1944, the majority of Jerry fighter attacks were made in mass formations. We called them gaggles. A formation of 15 to 50 109s or 190s would fly off one leader and fire simultaneously during the attack. The purpose of the tactic was an attempt to bring mass firepower to bear on a box of bombers. The principle was good, but the tactic poor. Indeed, the five 109s I got on one mission I plucked out of just such a formation."

—A tour-end report by Bill Whisner in early 1945.

Above: Bill Whisner runs through his pre-takeoff checks in *Moonbeam McSwine* at Bodney in 1944.

(continued from pg 92)

"I picked out a 190 and pressed the trigger. Nothing happened ... I reached down and turned on my gun switch and gave a couple of good bursts. As I watched him hit the ground and explode, I felt myself being hit. I broke sharply to the right and up. A 190 was about 50 yards behind me, firing away ... I had several 20 mm holes in each wing and another hit my oil tank. My left aileron was also out and I was losing oil, but pressure and temperature were still steady. Being over friendly territory, I could see no reason for landing immediately. I turned toward a big dogfight and soon had another 190 ... several 190s were in the vicinity so I engaged one. We fought for 5 or 10 minutes and I finally managed to get behind him ... he tumbled to the ground. Bandits were reported strafing the field ... I saw a 109. We made two head-on passes and on the second I hit him on the nose and wings. The 109 crashed and burned east of the strip. I chased several more but they evaded into cloud cover ... my windshield was covered in oil so I headed back and landed."

These were Whisner's final victories of World War II and he received a second D.S.C. for his bravery.

"As a boy lieutenant, I was coerced into giving the name Princess Elizabeth to my until-then nameless P-51B by an eager young PIO (Public Information Officer) from New York. Named in honor of "the" Elizabeth (later to be Queen Elizabeth), it was thought that favorable publicity would accrue to the group should I do some good things in combat in the 51. However, I immediately succumbed to the kidding and changed the name to what I considered the complete social antithesis—Moonbeam McSwine."

—Taken from a letter to author Tom Ivie from Bill Whisner, dated February 9, 1988.

MAJ. WILLIAM T. HALTON

352ND FIGHTER GROUP – "Blue-Nosed Bastards of Bodney"

William Halton, from Providence, Rhode Island, enlisted as an aviation cadet in August 1941 and received his wings and commission in March 1942. After a year of instructor duties, he was assigned to the 352nd FG and 328th FS at Mitchell Field, New York, where he flew a P-47. He shipped out with the group to Bodney, England, in June 1943. During August of that year, he was promoted to Captain. He participated in a documentary film called *Combat America*, and posed with the famous actor Clark Gable and a fellow pilot Dick DeBruin for a photograph. DeBruin sent the photograph home and his wife showed the picture to her ladies club. All the girls fell in love with Halton, not Gable.

Halton was declared combat ready in early September and participated as a flight leader in the uneventful first 352nd mission. He scored one Me109 and damaged a Ju-88 in a strafing run before he finished his first tour of duty in May 1944. He had converted from the P-47 to the P-51B in April. In August 1944, Halton returned to Bodney and the 328th, and flew a number of combat missions before he replaced Maj. George Preddy as Operations Officer in the 487th FS. Halton flew a new P-51D named *Slender, Tender, and Tall* and downed two 109s in November.

Based at Asch, Belgium, on December 26, 1944, he increased his aerial score to three Me109s. The following day he destroyed another 109, near Bonn, Germany. As he climbed back to join his Yellow Flight, he saw a 109 trio in loose Vic. "I pounced on the one on the extreme left and opened fire at 300 yards. I observed no strikes, but he crashed in the woods and blew up. Then I attacked the one on the right firing on him from 300 to 100 yards and observed many strikes around the engine and cockpit. I passed under him and observed the 109 burning fiercely around the engine and cockpit. I then attacked the lead ship and opened fire at 200 yards. I had only one gun firing then but observed strikes around the engine and he began to stream coolant and black smoke. Out of ammo, I called Lt. Goebel to finish him off. He attacked it and I watched the enemy aircraft crash and blow up in the woods."

He received a FW190 during the legendary New Year's Day *Luftwaffe* attack on Asch. On January 2, he replaced Lt. Col. Meyer as Squadron CO following the latter's unfortunate road accident. Later in the month he caught a 109 down low and blew it apart, and on March 18, he triumphed over another 109. His final World War II victories were a FW190 and an Me109 destroyed in airfield strafing at Plattling, Germany. He died in a Mustang during the Korean War.

"I lost my flight in the dive, and when I got back to 30,000 feet, I was quite alone in the midst of six Me109s. I found no trouble in out-turning them in my Mustang, and fought them for several minutes. I was unable to get a shot at any, as I had to break back into more of them as soon as I began to track one. The Huns did not seem too bright, as they kept turning in the Lufberry with me, instead of half of them breaking off and attacking from the other direction. After several minutes I was spotted by a flight of P-51s, and I dove down and joined them."

—Capt. Halton's encounter report for November 2, 1944. He was credited with a destroyed Bf109 on this mission, his second Bf109, of 10.5 kills.

Above: *Slender, Tender, and Tall* pictured at Bodney in 1945.

CAPT. RAYMOND H. LITTGE

352ND FIGHTER GROUP – "Blue-Nosed Bastards of Bodney"

ay Littge was from a family of eight children that was orphaned at an early age. By working as a farmhand after school and during the summer, he was able to raise enough cash to fulfill his dream of becoming a pilot.

With his hard-earned private pilot's license in hand, he joined the USAAC in July 1942 and was commissioned in December 1943. Six months later he was on his way to England to join the 487th FS, 352nd FG—the famous "Blue Nosers of Bodney."

On his first operational mission, the Squadron engaged a gaggle of Me109s, and scored one down and three damaged. By his seventh mission, he was involved in a Group battle that he recorded as follows, "Group got 21 enemy aircraft—Ju-88s and Me109s. My Flight Leader got two Me109s. Lots of excitement. Saw at least 75 enemy aircraft. Major Preddy got four. Ellison got three. Fowler got two—so fast I didn't even fire my guns—I was his wingman."

Littge opened his personal scoring in late August. After a bomber escort mission, his flight strafed Neuebrandenburg airfield, where he destroyed two Me210s and damaged a 109. "When we hit an airfield, we get down as low as possible. Right on the ground under trees, etc., and are doing 450 miles per hour. After hitting we usually keep right on going." In September, he got two parked Ju-88s by doing the same kind of strafing. On his 46th mission, he was tested in aerial combat and came out with two Me109s to his credit, and the scoring continued. He wrote to his fiancée Helen "… makes 12 victories now! Gee, when I came over here I thought to myself, 'Golly, I hope the *Luftwaffe* is not wiped out before I get a chance.'"

He racked up several more until his notable last aerial victory against an Me262 jet. Littge continued in combat until the end of hostilities and raised his total to 23.5 victories (both air and ground), including a spectacular six strafing kills in one mission, for which he was awarded a D.S.C. He was 21 years old when he went home a hero. The chance and random nature of survival during World War II is still evident through Capt. Littge's *Miss Helen*. Littge was killed due to a systems failure in a jet aircraft after the war, but *Miss Helen* passed through several owners—military and civilian—to ultimately survive and it is still flown in England.

Above: Ray Littge's gun camera film captured his Me262 kill on March 25, 1945.

"I kicked my tanks off and rolled over after him. My initial speed brought me to within a 1,000 yards of the 262, and I stayed there for a while. He gradually pulled away, and after about a 15-minute chase, he was out of sight. When I pulled up I was directly over Rechlin Airdrome, near Muritz Lake. After I circled Rechlin for about five minutes, an Me262 came over the field—presumably the one I had previously chased and peeled off. As he was lowering his wheels, I made a 90-degree pass at him, seeing no strikes. He leveled off and then I got behind him, fired several long bursts, and saw quite a few strikes, some of which set his right jet on fire. His evasive action consisted of gentle left and right turns. He then jettisoned his canopy, pulled up to 2,000 feet, and bailed out. His 'chute did not open."

—Capt. Littge's encounter report for March 25, 1945. He was credited with an Me262 kill on this day. This was his final victory of the war, with a final tally of 10.5 kills.

Above: Capt. Ray Littge on the wing of 44-72216, *Miss Helen*, with Assistant Crew Chief Sgt. Mohler.

"We had finished a pass through the bomber formation. There was nothing funny about these jet jobs, but this one was having trouble with his landing gear. It kept dropping down and reminded me of a kid who was running away from someone and whose pants kept dropping down. He was trying to fight, fly, and at the same time keep working his gear up. This factor decreased his speed and I was able to close up and clobber him."

—Lt. Ray Littge, Combat Report, Nov. 27, 1944. One Me262

352ND FIGHTER GROUP – "Blue-Nosed Bastards of Bodney"

Edwin Heller graduated from flight training in February 1943 and was sent to an Operational Training Unit at Westover, Massachusetts, where he flew the P-47. He joined the 21st FS, which was transformed into the 486th FS that was shipped out to England on the *Queen Elizabeth* during June 1943.

The first combat operations took place in the fall of 1943, and Heller drew first blood, albeit a shared German E-Boat off the coast of Belgium, in February 1944.

In April, the unit traded its P-47s for P-51Bs. The training consisted of twice around the patch at Bodney and two landings; the conversion was complete!

A mission on April 24 won Heller a D.S.C. During German airfield sweeps he destroyed two Ju-88s and an Me110 at Ingolstadt—despite the fact that his leader was downed by ground fire—and flamed three Me110s at Bokingen. At Creilsham, he got strikes on three 110s, set one on fire, and destroyed another in the take-off phase.

His first aerial victories came in early May 1944 near Hanover, where he downed an Me109 from 150 yards at 5,000 feet. Heller separated from his leader and hit another 109, which went into wild evasion at low level. "We got into a Lufberry at 130 miles per hour and I had 10 degrees of flap. He finally straight-

ened out and I noticed he was preparing to crash land as his engine was smoking badly. I gave him a last burst just as he hit the top of a bridge and went in the river. I took a picture … then returned by myself."

At the end of May, Heller scored another Me109 and one shared, this time at high altitude. In June, the aircraft participated in the Normandy landing then went to Russia with the first of the Shuttle missions. Heller made the record books by shooting down a 109 some 1,000 miles from base. His return from Russia was adventurous: first, he was delayed by a prop strike, which was followed by an engine change, then he flew alone to Tehran, then to Cairo, Benghazi, and Casablanca where an envious USAAF General commandeered his Mustang and put him on a transport to England.

It wasn't until Heller's second tour when he flew a P-51D, with his familiar *Hell-er-Bust* markings, that he scored again. Operating from the forward airfield at Chievres, Belgium, he downed an FW190 that had attacked U.S. bombers on a mission to Rositz, Germany.

The Blue-Nosers moved back to base at Bodney in the first half of April 1945. On a B-17 escort mission to Germany, Heller finished his scoring with an amazing strafing record, and claimed seven aircraft destroyed on the heavily defended Gonecker *Luftwaffe* airfield.

Right: *Hell-er Bust* PZ-H sits amid a crowded parking area on the Bodney field.

"I was flying Yellow three on the first leg of an escort mission to Russia. When the Jerries came in to attack the bombers from 11 o'clock high, we broke their bounce by making our pass at a four-ship flight of them from 3 o'clock. As Yellow leader was closing on the tail of a 109, I observed another Jerry queuing up on his tail. I immediately chased the Hun that was pursuing Yellow leader and forced him to break for the deck. I followed him down to about 8,000 feet where I finished him off with a burst from 200 yards dead astern. The Me109 poured out black smoke and the last I saw of the E/A was when it went into the ground. I claimed one Me109 destroyed."

—Lt. Ed Heller, Russian Shuttle Mission to Pyratin, June 21, 1944.

Above: *Hell-er Bust* is parked in front of a Suffolk tree line.

"I landed in Casablanca with the intention of getting new drop tanks and flying home via the coast of Portugal, France, and across the Bay of Biscay. However, the resident general had his eyes on my Hell-er-Bust and I was summarily grounded! Leaving my beloved P-51 in North Africa, I boarded a transport plane to England, and home."

—Quote from Lt. Heller's diary for June 1944. It relates to his struggle to get back to the U.K. after he participated in the first 8th Air Force Shuttle Mission to Russia. He returned to Bodney several weeks after his squadron mates in the 352nd FG, minus his Mustang.

May 28, 1944. Dessau area. Blue Flight lead by Capt. Woody Anderson. Spotting contrails above the bomber force, the Blue Flight, consisting of Anderson, Lt. Lester Howell, and Lt. Ed Heller, were bounced by 25 German fighters.

Heller said, "It was impossible to stay together, and Capt. Anderson tagged on to one and headed down on his tail while I took on another. By that time we were both in a fight and on our own. Lt. Lester Howell, Blue 2, saw Capt. Anderson get many good hits on his 109 before his attention was taken away by his own attack." Ed Heller destroyed a 109 and shared a second. Lt. Howell destroyed one 109.

Both men confirmed what was to be Capt. Anderson's last victory for a total of 13.5—4.5 aerial and 9 ground. Anderson bailed out of his crippled plane, but, tragically, his chute failed to open.

—Quote from 352nd Fighter Group History, "Blue-Nosed Bastards of Bodney."

Left: Ed Heller's crew chief points out to his boss the battle damage collected during combat.

CHAPTER 6

354TH FIGHTER GROUP – "Pioneer Mustang Group"

353rd, 355th, and 356th Fighter Squadron

The 354th's place in history is assured. They were the first group to operate the Mustang in the European Theater of Operations (ETO). Founded in November of 1942, the 354th FG shipped out to Britain on the *Athlone Castle* in October 1943. Based initially at Greenham Common in Berkshire—where pilots were trained in the new P-51Bs—the 354th moved to its operational airfield at Boxted. By November, the group was in action on bomber escort duties over occupied France.

Re-assigned to the 9th AF, the 354th stayed at Boxted until April 1944, and flew principally as defensive escort for bomber sorties into France and Germany. During that period, Maj. Jim Howard of the 356th FS (an ex-Flying Tiger) brought distinction to the Group and won the only Medal of Honor awarded to a U.S. pilot in the ETO. He single-handedly fought off 30 enemy fighters, and downed three of them.

Bomber escort missions changed to tactical training when the Group moved to Lashenden, a forward airfield in the south of England, in preparation for the D-Day landings in Normandy. By July 9, the Group was based only 10 miles from the front at Criqueville in Northern France. From there it transferred to a former *Luftwaffe* base at Gael, in Brittany, where the Group celebrated the destruction of its 500th enemy aircraft.

In September, the 354th moved forward again to Orconte in the Champagne country where it gave up its trusty Mustangs for P-47s, prior to the Battle of the Bulge, the Rhine crossings, and the occupation of Germany.

The 354th FG scored a total of 957 confirmed kills, 53 probables, and 428 damaged. In its 1,384 missions, 187 of its pilots were lost, killed, or MIA. The 354th's aces roster included Capt. Kenneth Dahlberg, Lt. Col. Glenn Eagleston, and Capt. Richard Turner.

Right: Lt. Bruce W. Carr poses in P-51D, *Angel's Playmate*, 44-63497.

LT. BRUCE W. CARR

354TH FIGHTER GROUP – "Pioneer Mustang Group"

ruce Carr shot down his first aircraft, an Me109, on March 8, 1944. His recognition came by means of an admonishment for being over-aggressive. Carr considered this an insult and became a rebel. As a result of his insubordination, he was scheduled to be court-martialed. Fortunately, this came to the attention of Capt. Glen Eagleston of the 354th FG, who inspired Carr's transfer to his 353rd FS. Despite the fact that Carr became one of the units aces and often led missions, it took him over a year to be promoted from Flight Officer to Second Lieutenant.

When the group supported the D-Day landings, Carr shared a FW190 and was credited with a probable Me109. One of his big days came on September 12th over Germany. Carr led his flight down on to seven parked Ju-88 bombers and flamed two before he climbed back up to altitude. They spotted 30-plus FW190s about 2,000 feet below. He picked-off one, which then exploded. Carr saw a loner running from the fight at low level, nailed him during a left turn, and witnessed the stricken aircraft snap onto its back and plunge into a hill.

His report continues, "I then climbed back up to about 6,000 feet where I saw a FW190 diving for the deck 80 degrees from the way I was going. I turned right and shot a very short burst at 80 degrees deflection from 200 yards. I saw hits all around the cockpit. The enemy aircraft steepened its dive, rolled over on his back and went in. The pilot did not get out … I then climbed back up to about 10,000 feet and ran into 20-plus Me109s. There were too many for me and I saw a lone P-51 below them smoking. I was afraid they would bounce him so I went down to give him cover."

In October, Carr's unit was bounced from front and rear by over 70 Me109s. In the ensuing melee, which was fought right down to the deck, he managed to down two of them. With no further fights until year-end, Carr took leave in the states and returned to the squadron in March. During a mess party, one of the unit's new-comers bet a drunken Carr $1,000 that he could not down an enemy aircraft on the first mission after his return. Carr could not afford to lose.

The squadron cruised the Eiffel Tower area without joy, and when it turned for Munich, Carr saw two FW190s in close formation. He issued strict instructions to the rest of the unit not to fire until he had nailed the leader. Carr's aim was true and the FW190 exploded and burst into flames. The subdued Lieutenant bought the bar that night. "War is hell because I have yet to collect the bet I could not afford to lose," he later recalled.

Carr went on to become an "ace in a day" on April 2, when he downed three FW190s and two Me109s over Nuremberg. The "over-aggressive" pilot finished the war with a score of 14 destroyed, three probables, and 7.5 ground kills.

Above: Bruce Carr carried out a low pass in the FW190 he stole from a Luftwaffe base in Czechoslovakia. He bellied the German fighter in when he could not lower the gear.

"I closed directly behind the lead aircraft with about a 50 miles per hour overtake. It was hard not to fire as soon as we were within range but I not only wanted to destroy the lead aircraft, I wanted to do it in front of the Squadron with a minimum of bullet expenditure. At about 150 feet, I fired a short burst. The lead 190 exploded and burst into flames."

—Lt. Carr's encounter report for March 9, 1945. He was credited with an FW190 long-nose destroyed on this day. This victory took his tally to 7.5 kills and "won" him a $1,000 bet that he had made the night before at the bar, but never collected.

Above: Carr's Focke Wulf becomes the center of attention right after his unbelievable escape and evasion.

CHAPTER 7

357TH FIGHTER GROUP – "Yoxford Boys"

362nd, 363rd, and 364th Fighter Squadrons

The 357th FG left its stateside training bases and P-39 Airacobras in November 1943, and left for England. The Group exchanged the relative discomfort of a winter sea crossing in the *Queen Elizabeth* (then outfitted to sail with 15,000 troops), for a sea of mud at the newly constructed Raydon Wood airfield in Suffolk. Only two months later, the 1,000-man team and its new P-51B Mustangs were pushed out by the 358th FG (a P-47 outfit), and moved to Leiston, where it remained until the end of the European conflict.

Leiston was three miles from the East Coast of England and just 80 miles across the inhospitable North Sea to German-occupied Holland. Near the village of Yoxford, Suffolk, the 357th at Leiston became famous as the red-and-yellow-nosed "Yoxford Boys," and were given regular mention by the notorious "Lord Haw Haw," a Nazi propaganda broadcaster.

Among the first U.S. 8th AF units to fly the Mustang in combat, the 357th was also the first to put Allied fighters over Berlin. They also conducted flights to Russia, over Romania and Italy. This was all in addition to the "milk run" missions over Germany, Holland, Benelux, and France.

Given the Group's primary task of the "Little Friend" bomber escort, it is not a surprise that it encountered large numbers of enemy fighters and was able to claim over 600 destroyed in a total of 313 missions. Strafing opportunities were also not missed, and more than 100 Axis aircraft were destroyed on the ground.

The legendary Leonard "Kit" Carson, Bud Anderson, Don Bochay, and Chuck Yeager were among the Group's most prolific aces. By the end of World War II, it had 43 aces in its alumni, the largest in the 8th Air Force.

Even with all of these accomplishments, one should never forget the human cost of such efforts. From this Group alone, 144 aircraft fell in action, 73 pilots died from combat, and 13 were killed in training accidents.

Right: A gaggle of 357th FG Mustangs on a training flight over England in 1944.

357TH FIGHTER GROUP – "Yoxford Boys"

Bud Anderson joined the USAAF as a cadet in early 1942, and by the end of the year, was assigned to the 328th FG that flew P-39s out of his Oakland, California, birthplace, in defense of San Francisco. A few months later, Anderson joined the newly formed 363rd FS, 357th FG, equipped with Airacobras, at Tonapah, Nevada.

The group went to England in late-1943 and became the first 8th AF unit to operate the P-51B Mustang. It was not long before he encountered the *Luftwaffe*. "I'm turning with this 109 now, northwest of Hanover. We're flying interlocking circles but on different planes. Descending, we pass each other once, twice, three times at ridiculous angles … I'm cocky enough to try something bizarre. I decide to pull my sights through the German, keeping my nose up until I can't see him, then fire, hose him and hope against all odds that he flies through the stream. What the hell. Worth a try. I pull up and around and fire off a quick stream of tracer as he disappears beneath me. And another for luck. I ease the stick back and he flies into my view. *Hot Damn!* He's spilling coolant back into his slipstream. I got him! Got a golden goddamned B-B on him! Got my first kill! And whilst I'm whooping, he throws the canopy off and bails out. My crew checked the four guns. Of the 1,260 rounds of ammo available on the P-51B, I had used only 50—or, putting that into trigger time, less than one second's worth."

Bud named his aircraft *Old Crow* after a whiskey he favored. In more politically correct times, he said that he had named it after the smartest bird in the air!

Escort missions to targets all over Germany offered opportunities for Bud to hone his skills against determined defenses by FW190s and Me109s. Despite a vacation in the United States between the summer and fall of 1944, Anderson ended his World War II service with 16 aerial victories and one aircraft destroyed on the ground.

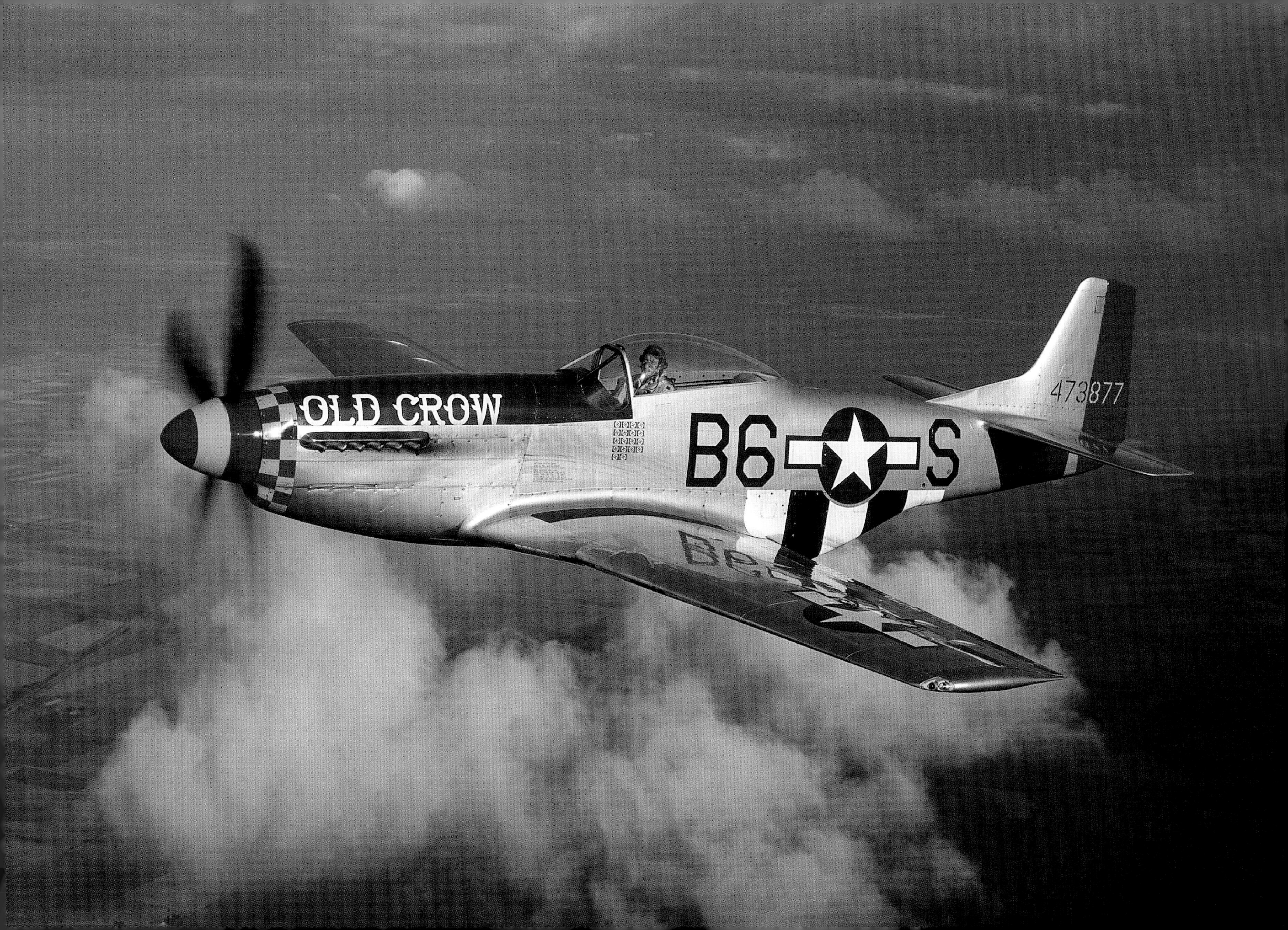
OLD CROW
B6 S
473877

"The P-51 was pleasant and forgiving to fly. Best of all, it went like hell. The Merlin had great gobs of power, and was equally at home high or low, thanks to the two-stage, two-speed supercharger. We sensed it was special, even before we measured it against what the enemy pilots were flying."

–Capt. Bud Anderson, 357th FG.

Top: P-51B *Old Crow* 43-24823.
Above: P-51D *Old Crow* 44-41450.

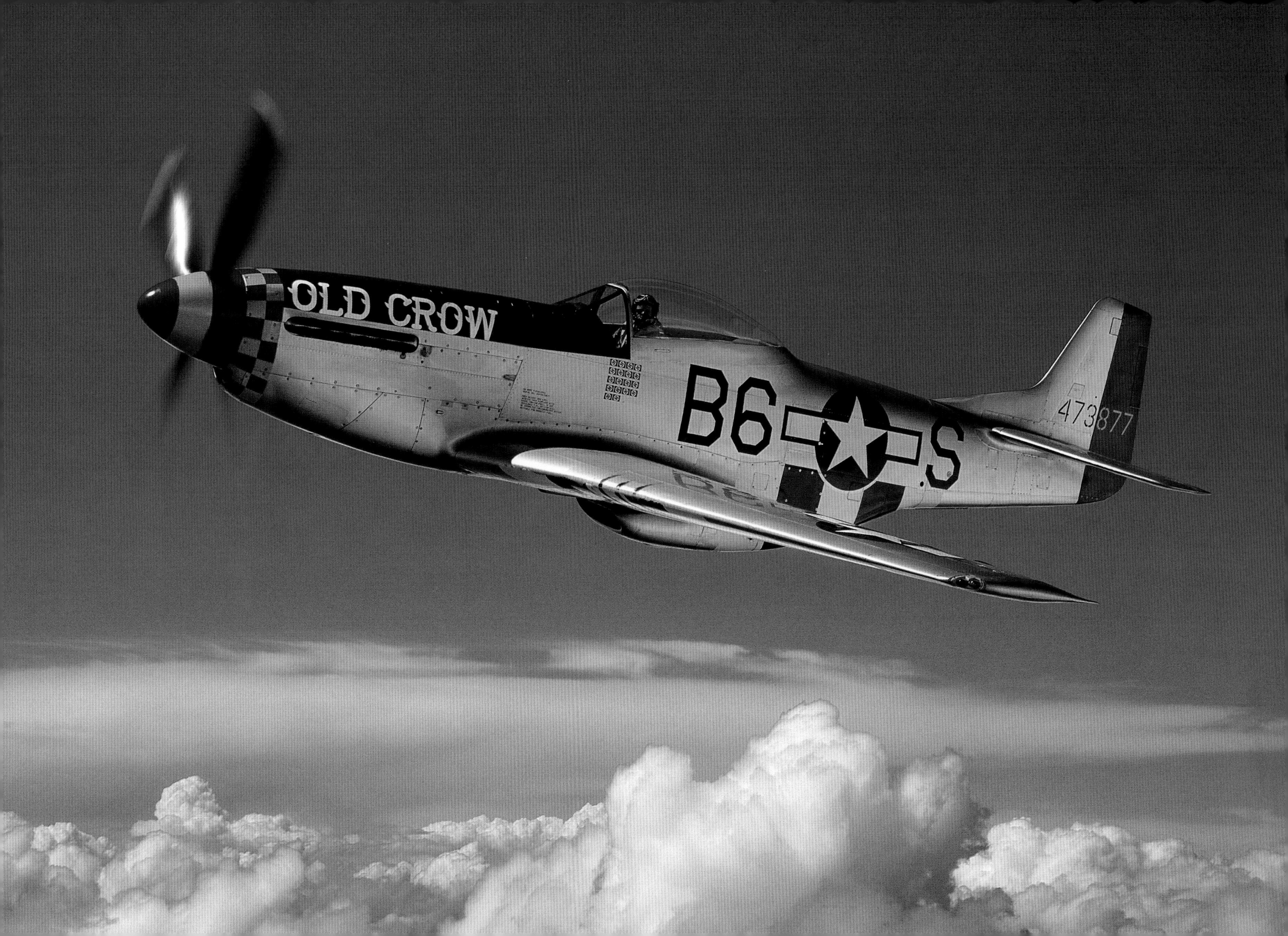
OLD CROW
B6
S
473877

"We descended five miles and then ran out of sky. He lit out across the fields, hedge-hopping, with me and my wingman behind him. As I closed in to fire, he must have looked back, probably terrified now, and inadvertently shoved forward maybe an inch on the stick. At that height and speed, an inch would have been more than enough. The Messerschmitt simply flew into the ground at full power and blew up like a bomb."

—Taken from *To Fly and Fight – Memoirs of a Triple Ace* by Col. Clarence E. 'Bud' Anderson

Left: Four of the 357th FG's top scorers (left to right), Pete Peterson, Kit Carson, Johnny England, and Bud Anderson.

CAPT. CHARLES "CHUCK" YEAGER

357TH FIGHTER GROUP – "Yoxford Boys"

Born in the West Virginian Appalachian Mountains, Yeager was taught how to hunt and shoot, and the experience paid off during his combat career. After training on the P-39 (said to be his favorite airplane), and then on the P-47, he shipped out with the 357th FG on the *Queen Elizabeth*. The eventual destination was Leiston in East Anglia, where the group had its long-term base.

Yeager's first score was on an escort mission to Berlin on March 4, 1944, when he got the better of an Me109. Unfortunately, the very next day the roles were reversed when he was shot down by a FW190. "After only eight combat missions, I'm now MIA. World War II shot out from under me by the 20 mm cannons of a Focke Wulf 190. The world exploded. I ducked to protect my face with my hands, and when I looked a second later, my engine was on fire and there was a gaping hole in my wingtip. The airplane began to spin. It happened so fast … my burning P-51 began to snap and roll, heading for the ground." Yeager successfully bailed out, was lightly wounded, and landed in the woods bordering Angouleme, in the region of Bordeaux, Western France. He was studying his silk escape map when a forester stumbled upon him. Luckily, the forester took Yeager to see an elderly lady who arranged for the French Resistance Maquis to help him escape over the Pyrenees to Spain. Via the U.S. Consul, Gibraltar, and the RAF, Yeager was back in Leiston by the middle of May and

pushed to stay in combat. General Eisenhower himself empowered the stay.

Yeager occasionally led the group, despite the fact he was only a Lieutenant, in *Glamorous Glennis*, the P-51D named after his future wife. He picked out 22 Me109s circling to intercept the B-24s they were escorting. "They did not see us coming at them out of the sun … I came in behind their tail-end Charlie … when he suddenly broke left and ran into his wingman. They both bailed out. It was almost comic, scoring two quick victories without firing a shot. By now all the airplanes in the sky had dropped their tanks and were spinning and diving in a wild, wide-open dogfight. I blew up a 109 from 600 yards—my third victory—when I turned around and saw another angling in behind me. Man, I pulled back on my throttle so dammed hard I nearly stalled, rolled up and over, came in behind and under him, kicking right rudder, and simultaneously firing. I was directly underneath the guy, less than 50 feet, and I opened up that 109 as if it were a can of Spam. That made four. A moment later, I waxed a guy's fanny in a steep dive; I pulled up at about 1,000 feet; he went straight into the ground."

Yeager also shot down two Me262s and a series of FW190s. "I loved to dogfight. It was a clean contest of skill, stamina, and courage, one on one." Yeager finished the war with 11.5 aerial victories. He went on to gain immortal fame when he became the first pilot to break the sound barrier.

"Many of our P-51s flew 50 straight missions without an abort, and my crew chief got a Bronze Star for his work. I flew the P-47, P-38, Bf109, FW190, Spitfire, and several other lesser-known types, and the P-51D was by far the best war machine. The Mustang would do for eight hours what the Spit would do for 45 minutes! For me, the D-model was the definitive article, for it solved all the problems that we had experienced with the P-51B. Indeed, the only bad flight characteristic (of both models) came about when the fuselage tank was full. This wasn't exactly dangerous, but one had to be careful when turning. We were glad to see the back of the P-51B, with its four guns and bad ammunition feed."

—Capt. Chuck Yeager

Above: P-51D *Glamorous Glen III* 44-14888, Winter 1944.

LT. COL. THOMAS "TOMMY" LLOYD HAYES

357TH FIGHTER GROUP – "Yoxford Boys"

Born in 1917 in Portland, Oregon, Thomas "Tommy" Hayes attended the State University and left to become a Flight Cadet in June 1940. He received his wings at Kelly Field, Texas, in February 1941, and was assigned to the 35th Pursuit Group, 70th Pursuit Squadron. With a total flight time of 518 hours, Hayes was posted to the Pacific Theater, with the 17th PS in Java. He was shot down in a P-40 during February 1942. After Hayes recovered from his wounds, he was transferred to the 35th FG in New Guinea where he obtained two ground victories in the P-39. He was rotated back to the United States in October 1942 and assigned to fighter training duties.

In October 1943 Hayes was promoted to Major and assigned to command the 364th FS, 357th FG, which shipped out to Leiston, Suffolk, in Eastern England.

His first aerial victories were obtained in a P-51B in February and March of 1944, when he downed a succession of Me109s, an Me410, and an Me110 over Northern Germany. He was the first ace in the group. In May 1944, he was promoted to Lieutenant Colonel and had some serious fun around D-Day. Hayes lobbed full drop tanks at ammo trains in France and gunned them into explosion!

On June 29, 1944, Hayes led the group on an escort mission, and flew his new P-51D 44-13318, C5-N nicknamed *Frenesi*. That day, the 357th shot down 20 enemy aircraft in the Leipzig area, and Hayes claimed an Me109 and shared an Me410. After high G circling for some time with the 109 for some time, the combat came to a close when Hayes pulled through and got a burst in. The damaged 109 split S, with Hayes in his six as they went through the clouds. The German fighter flamed on hitting the deck, while Hayes pulled hard and climbed out to seek his wingman.

On July 25, his combat report reads, "Intercepted 25-plus Me109s and FW190s attacking unidentified P-38 at 20,000 feet at 11:50. Group engaged these enemy aircraft which dove for the deck over Paris. Combat was from 8,000 feet to Paris rooftops." Hayes' pilots felled five of the *Luftwaffe's* best with no losses.

Lt. Col. Hayes finished his participation in World War II with 10.5 aerial scores plus the two Japanese ground victories.

Above: *Frenesi* P-51D (model D-5) on its hardstand at Leiston during the summer of 1944.
Right: Tommy Hayes with his very proud ground crew. Hayes was the Deputy Group Commanding Officer at the time this photo was taken.

PILOT
LT.COL. THOMAS L. HAYES
CREW CHIEF
S/SGT. ROBERT L. KRULL
ASS'T. CREW CHIEF
SGT. GENE J. BARBALOU
ARMORER
SGT. FRED KEIPER

"There was no cloud cover in the area, but the Germans had smoke generators all around Berlin, and the smoke was up to 15,000 feet. Even though I was closing on it, the 109 became obscured in the smoke, and then it disappeared altogether. I pulled out at about 15,000 feet. As I pulled around to look for the 109—or anyone else—something went by, straight down. Then, all of a sudden, something else went down, and by this time I could identify it. It was a stick of 500-pound bombs. It looked like a ladder going straight down-all rungs and no rails. I was in the wrong place! I looked around, and there were plenty more ladders. I looked up and all I could see were four-engine bombers. Holy God! Bombers were over me and Berlin was under me! I was thinking, 'Which way do I turn?' I kicked the airplane and snap-rolled straight down. At least now I was parallel to the falling bombs. Heading for the closest rural area off to the West, I started back up."

—Lt. Col. Tommy Hayes from an interview with Eric Hammel, in Aces Against Germany

CAPT. RICHARD A. "PETE" PETERSON

357TH FIGHTER GROUP – "Yoxford Boys"

Richard Peterson left his native Minnesota for the Aviation Cadet Program in March 1942. With his wings and new commission, he joined the 364th FS at Tonapah, Nevada, where he developed his fighter skills on the Bell P-39 Airacobra. In November 1943, he shipped out to England, where the 357th was the first 8th AF Fighter Group equipped with the P-51B.

Initial combat missions were flown in February 1944. In March, Peterson's opening score was with a FW190 near Bordeaux, and the falling German pilot saluted him! Peterson shared an Me110 over Munich on March 16, and two days later, he downed an Me109, followed by two others on April 11 and 24. He made ace by April 30, when he downed another Me109 and a FW190. On May 12, he claimed an Me410 and shared another near Poznan in Poland. This victory was followed later in the month by another Me109 that fell to his guns over Magdeburg.

On July 1, in his P-51D *Hurry Home Honey* (named from the way his wife finished letters to him), he picked up a pair of 109s during a patrol over St. Quentin, France. Peterson fired at one as it disappeared into the clouds, and he ducked below to see if he could cut off its escape, only to find it in a vertical dive and smashing into the ground. Peterson then heard a call for help and saw a 357th Mustang in a Lufbery circle with a 109 in hot pursuit. Peterson opened fire and the Messerschmitt flew into the ground and exploded. Thereafter, Peterson was sent home on leave and returned for a second tour in time for a fight over Berlin on Oc-

tober 6, 1944. He claimed one 190, whose pilot bailed without a shot being fired. Peterson picked off a 109 with guns the following day.

His final scores were a 190 over Meerseburg, and a 109 that he nailed in the climb when he led his squadron over the Neuhausen airfield. In two combat tours he flew 118 missions, scored 15.5 aerial victories, and 3.5 enemy aircraft on the ground.

"There was a Red Cross gal on the base named Ginny Curnutt. She was the only American girl at Leiston among several thousand American men, and damned attractive. At a reunion in Denver 35 years later, she showed up with a tablecloth we'd all written on at my tour-end going-away party in July 1944. "Ginny", I'd scrawled, "thanks for the <u>swell</u> party!" She asked Pete Peterson if he recalled what he'd written, which gave Pete a bad moment, since he'd been rather committed at the time to the girl he would marry, Elaine ... and Mrs. Peterson was there in Denver, right on his arm. Given the circumstances, and the amount of liquor that had flowed that night at Leiston, anyone might have written damn near anything to coax a smile from sweet Ginny. She showed Pete the tablecloth. "Hurry Home Honey", he'd scrawled. It was the name of his Mustang."

—Lt. Col. Bud Anderson

Left: Hollis "Bud" Nowlin, Mark Stepelton, Pete Peterson, and Louis Fecher; all 364th FS pilots during the fall of 1944.

"Fifty to 75 enemy aircraft hit the box of bombers behind the one we were escorting. We immediately dropped our tanks and turned to engage them. I spotted an FW190 and gave chase. He was quite a bit below me, and I got too damned eager. I closed in on him as he leveled out at about 5,000 feet. I realized I was over-running him and lowered flaps as I pulled up alongside him. He looked over at me, jettisoned his canopy, and bailed out!"

—Capt. Peterson's encounter report for October 6, 1944. He was credited with a destroyed FW190 on this day for a total of 11.5 kills.

Above: *Little Friend.* **Pete Peterson flew a B-17 over the North Sea to the base.**

MAJ. DONALD H. BOCHKAY

357TH FIGHTER GROUP – "Yoxford Boys"

on Bockay was an infantryman with the 7th Division when he applied for flight training in 1941. He gained his Wings in 1943, was assigned to the 357th FG, and shipped out to Leiston in East Anglia with the 363rd FS, and flew the P-51B.

His first victory came on March 5, 1944, and was a shared FW190. The next day was more eventful as he managed to bag a pair of Me110s that were attacking B-17s over Berlin. His Mustang was named *Speedball Alice* and had a winged ace of spades on the left upper engine cowl, added when he followed up with three Me109s in the month of April. In June and July he scored two FW190s and an Me109 over France. He scored again against a FW190 over Merseberg, Germany, before he took leave in the United States.

Bockay returned to his buddies in 363rd FS before the turn of the year and quickly got in the groove and took out two more 190s near Berlin on December 5, 1944. In early February 1945, a flight of nine Me262 jet fighters swept in to attack bombers being escorted by the 363rd FS in the area of Fulda, Germany. The Mustangs were able to place themselves in between the formations, and one of the 262s fell to the P-51D adorned with the winged ace of spades.

Bockay had become one of the rare Allied pilots to score against the German jets and received a second on April 18, in the vicinity of Prague, Czechoslovakia, when he sighted a 262. "I dropped my tanks and dove from 15,000 to 13,000 feet, pulling up behind the Me262. I then let him have a burst from 400 yards, getting very good hits on his right jet unit and canopy. He then broke right in a very tight diving turn, pulling streamers from his wing tips. My G meter read 9 Gs. As he straightened out at 7,000 feet, I was 250 yards behind him going about 475 miles per hour. I let him have another burst, getting very good hits on his right jet unit again. He then popped his canopy as I let him have another burst; large pieces came off his ship, and it caught fire. I pulled off to miss the pieces and watched the Me262 fall apart. His tail came off. It then rolled over and went in like a torch."

Bockay completed two tours with 123 combat sorties, 510 combat hours, and was credited with 13.8 victories

Above: Bomber liaison. If the group wasn't flying on Operations, they were on training missions. On a perfect English summer's day, Don Bochkay leads a flight of three Mustangs on fighter affiliation work with the 8th Air Force B-24 Liberator.

"The lead 262 headed straight down. The one I hit broke to the left in a gentle turn, so I opened up on him again at about 400 yards and kept firing all the way in on him. I saw many strikes all over him, and his canopy shattered, with large chunks flying off. I broke to the left to keep from running into him. As I passed, I spotted the pilot halfway out of his cockpit. The ship rolled over and the pilot fell out. He never opened his chute and the plane went straight in."

—Capt. Bochkay's encounter report for February 9, 1945. He was credited with a downed Me262 destroyed on this day for a total of 12.8 kills.

Above: Blister hangar night service on 357th Mustangs.

FLT. LT. JACK CLELAND, RNZAF

357TH FIGHTER GROUP – "Yoxford Boys"

J ack Cleland volunteered for the Royal New Zealand Air Force in March 1941 and flew Tiger Moths and Vincents from Harewood and Woodbourne. Four months later, he obtained his Brevet and was sent to England for advanced training on Miles Masters and Hurricanes. In June 1942 he was posted to No. 616 South Yorkshire Auxiliary Squadron and flew the high-altitude Spitfire VIs against the Ju-86P and Do217.

After nine months with No. 616 Squadron, Cleland received a short posting to North Africa, an assignment that proved fruitful as he met his future wife Isabel, a member of an ENSA troupe, on the ship back to England. After a fighter reconnaissance training course at Hawarden, he returned to 616 in December 1943 as a newly promoted Flight Lieutenant. In June 1944, in a Spitfire VII, he attacked and destroyed two FW190s over a *Luftwaffe* base at Laval, France. His aircraft was hit by flak in the wing, cockpit, and engine, and he tried to nurse it back to England, but was forced to bail out into the Channel south of Selsey Bill, where he was picked up by Air Sea Rescue within 15 minutes.

The next month, Cleland was attached to the U.S. 8th Air Force's 363rd Fighter Squadron based at Leiston. In a very short time he flew a personalized P-51D, B6-V, adorned with *Isabel III* and two victory crosses below the cockpit.

Cleland's bomber escort missions in the P-51 included overflights to Pyratin in Russia and the Ploesti, Romania, raids that overflew to Severo in Italy. Cleland returned to No. 616 Squadron in October 1944, but was quickly transferred to an Operational Training Unit until the end of hostilities.

CHAPTER 8

361ST FIGHTER GROUP – "Yellowjackets"

374th, 375th, and 376th Fighter Squadron

The 361st Group was activated at Richmond Army Base in Virginia, in February 1943. Its pilots started training on P-47 Thunderbolts at Langley Field in May 1943, and were shipped out to England in November of that year to the RAF base in Bottisham, Cambridgeshire, where they still flew Jugs.

In January 1944 the Group carried out its first offensive missions over France and Northern Germany. It was re-equipped in May with P-51Bs. Sadly, Lt. Eugene Kinnard was the first casualty, and was killed in a mock dogfight with an RAF Hurricane.

The Group successfully carried out a wide variety of escort and strafing missions in the build up to D-Day, but lost three pilots to ground fire in six missions on the first day of the Normandy invasion. Thereafter, it roamed widely over France, the Low Countries, and Germany. During September 1944, the 361st FG moved the few miles from Bottisham to Little Walden, Essex. In October, it had the distinction of being the first Group to shoot down German jets when Lt. Urban Drew of the 375th FS shot down a pair of Me262s as they took off from a base at Achmer in Germany.

In February 1945, the Group joined forward tactical units on the Continent, and was based at St Dizier, France, and Chievres, Belgium where it supported troops engaged in the Battle of the Ardennes. The 361st moved back to Little Walden in mid-April and escorted heavy bombers over the Third Reich and into Czechoslovakia. By V-E Day, the Group had claimed 266 destroyed airborne and 105 on the ground, for the loss of 81 Mustangs.

LT. URBAN "BEN" DREW

361ST FIGHTER GROUP – "Yellowjackets"

Drew had amassed some 700 hours in Mustangs as a Flight Instructor, and was highly frustrated to not be involved in the air war. After he buzzed a troop parade, he received his chance for combat and was transferred just after D-Day to Bottisham, England, as a replacement in the 361st FG, a unit that had lost a lot of young pilots (MIA) over France.

Several of the pilots at Bottisham were his ex-students. Some had been promoted in the field to captain or major, but they still charmingly called 2nd Lt. Drew, "Sir."

Drew was quick to make his mark in combat. His confidence and experience with the Mustang showed through. His third victory over an Me109 came when he saw a flight of P-38s being attacked by a gaggle of 109s. Drew reversed into a hammerhead stall to get behind one of them, and was spotted by a German adversary who powered into a tight spiraling dive from over 20,000 feet with Drew in close pursuit. Going through 10,000 feet, Drew thought, 'Is this guy better than me? I have to get it out of my mind, otherwise the wrong mother's son is going home tonight.' Closer to the deck, Drew kept some altitude on the 109, and despite the high G, managed to nail him in the pull out. "I felt very bad … here was one great fighter pilot … by God he could fly that Messerschmitt."

Drew had spotted a German jet fighter for the first time on a mission near the Czech border, but a chase proved futile. U.S. Intelligence said it could not divulge classified information on the German jet fighter, but Drew found out from a British source that the jets were based at Lechfeld and Achmer. October 7, 1944, found Drew in his Mustang *Detroit Miss* in flight over Achmer with his wingman Lt. Robert McCandless, when they spotted two Me262 Schwalbes commencing their take-off roll. The Mustang pair dived in on them and the first 262 exploded from the hail of Drew's 0.50 calibers. The second tried to climb away, but Drew got inside the turn and shot the tail off the jet which spun into the ground. After the gunfire had ceased, Drew noticed he was alone. McCandless had fallen to flak. It wasn't until after the war that Drew found out his wingman had survived.

On arrival at base, Drew's gun camera was broken, and without that evidence, or the witness of his wingman, the two victories could not be confirmed. Nearly 50 years later, a USAF clerk decided to contact the *Luftwaffe* records office. Hans-Peter Eder confirmed that he aborted his lead of JG7 that day, and he saw the two ill-fated Me262s taken out on take-off by a yellow-nosed Mustang. This was sufficient evidence to corroborate Drew's 1944 combat report. He was awarded a D.S.C. for the first allied victory over German jets some 40 years after the attack.

"I caught up with the second Me262 when he was about 1,000 feet off the ground. I was indicating 450 miles per hour, and the jet could not have been going faster than 200 miles per hour. I started firing from about 400 yards, 20 degrees deflection, and as I closed on him, I observed hits all over the wings and fuselage. Just as I passed him I saw a sheet of flame burst out near the right wing root. As I glanced back I saw a gigantic explosion, and a sheet of red-orange flame that shot out over the area from 1,000 feet."

–Lt. Drew's encounter report for October 7, 1944. He was credited with two destroyed Me262s on this day. These were his final kills of the war, and they took his tally to six kills.

TWILIGHT BREAK

It had been a long day. All day.

The Florida sky was in luminescent twilight. The first stars eased their way from heavenly anonymity to pierce the purple atmosphere. Crickets serenaded the onset of dusk; their lullaby soothed the senses on this balmy spring evening. Then growing quiet, but rising through their song, came another note. Another song. This increasing hum assumed a roar that carried high on the winds. An unmistakable roar that drew the trained ear from its earthbound limits. I was roused from my motel room to a west-facing balcony, joined by another figure familiar with that sound. As the rising crescendo took on an almost disturbing urgency, the source finally revealed itself. A perfect "Finger Four" of P-51 Mustangs powered into view, and in gorgeous coordination, they broke formation and peeled away one by one. Each aircraft glinted a brilliant gold high up in the sun's dying rays.

These Mustangs, named after the wild prarie horse, had travelled across the United States to attend the Gathering of Mustangs and Legends at Kissimmee, Florida, in 1999.

Organized by Stallion 51 Corporation, the event garnered sixty nine of these legendary beasts and 12 of the most famous pairs of hands to tame them. Amongst the honored few were Col. Bud Anderson, and Gen. Chuck Yeager.

It was at that meet that the idea for this book was born, and that moment of the twilight break embraced the three people that made it possible.

Norman Lees, a British P-51 pilot who flew cameraship countless times for me for more than 10 years, had traveled from the U.K. to help me photograph this remarkable event. Norman's devotion, friendship, and passion for the art of aerial photography allowed me to develop and do the work I love. Together we came up with the idea for this volume. We lost Norman Lees in April 2000 in a Spitfire training accident. You can imagine how I feel that he will never see it. Therefore, I'm dedicating this book to Norman, a friend and my inspiration.

The third individual was Stephen Grey, aloft in that four-ship formation, He'd brought those P-51s all the way from California. I wish he knew what that moment looked like from the ground in fact with the suns rays dying on the runway, I bet he wished that too!! Stephen is the driving force behind The Fighter Collection (TFC) based at the former World War II airfield in Duxford, England. TFC is the greatest existing collection of flying warbirds. The collection flourishes each year at the Flying Legends air show at the air field in Cambridgeshire, and it sets the standard for events worldwide.

Stephen's ability behind the stick is only matched by the power of his pen, knowledge, and observation. The words in this book are his tribute to the men and machines of World War II. The images are a collection of the finest black-and-white archive images along with my contemporary photography of 26 of the best and most accurately painted surviving P-51s. The idea or concept is simply to help take you to another time and place. These beautifully restored aircraft are tributes to the exceptional generation who went before us.

The color photographs have been compiled over five years and were shot in much the same way as they would have been when the Mustang was frontline hardware. They are real, and were not created on a computer. People in aviation have to deliver the very best they can, and I believe that the photographer should work by that ethic too, hence, everything here is genuine.

I hope you enjoy this book as much as I enjoyed watching the P-51s arrive that evening. It has been an incredible adventure and one that has enabled me to share the company and friendship of the special breed of people that created the P-51 legend, both then and now. It has been an honor.

Keep watching the skies for flying legends.

—*John Dibbs*
April 2002

'WD-C'
Pilot: *Aubrey Hair*
Operator:
Cavanaugh Flight Museum

'Shangri-La'
Pilot: *Brad Hood*
Operator:
C Osborn/Vintage Fighters

'Man O'War'
Pilot: *Bruce Guberman*
Operator:
E Ward/Square One Aviation

'Donald Duck'
Pilot: *Bob Tullius*
Operator:
R C Tullius/Group 44

'Sizzlin' Liz'
Pilot: *Dave Marco*
Operator:
D Marco/Barnstorm Aviation

'Ridgerunner'
Pilot: *Dan Martin*
Operator:
Dan Martin

'American Beauty'
Pilot: *Lee Lauderback*
Operator:
M Chapman/Stallion 51

'Flying Dutchman'
Pilot: *Brian Adams*
Operator:
Brian Adams

'Big Beautiful Doll'
Pilot: *Ed Shipley*
Operator:
Ed Shipley

'Big Beautiful Doll'
Pilot: *Mark Hanna*
Operator:
Old Flying Machine Co

'Worry Bird'
Pilot: *Mike George*
Operator:
M George/Air Combat Mus.

'Petie 3rd'
Pilot: *Pete McManus*
Operator:
Pete McManus

'Sweetie Face'
Pilot: *Tom Patten*
Operator:
Tom Patten

'Cripes A' Mighty 3rd'
Pilot: *Lee Lauderback*
Operator
K Weeks/Fantasy of Flight

'Princess Elizabeth'
Pilot: *Stephen Grey*
Operator:
The Fighter Collection

'Moonbeam McSwine'
Pilot: *Vlado Lenoch*
Operator:
Vlado Lenoch

'Slender, Tender & Tall'
Pilot: *Lee Lauderback*
Operator
T Blair/Stallion 51

'Miss Helen'
Pilot: *Pete John*
Operator:
Robs Lamplough

'Hell-er Bust'
Pilot: *Lee Lauderback*
Operator:
R Jepson/Stallion 51

'Angel's Playmate'
Pilot: *Lee Lauderback*
Operator:
J Newsome/Stallion 51

'Old Crow'
Pilot: *Bud Anderson*
Operator:
Jack Roush

'Old Crow'
Pilot: *Ray Hanna*
Operator:
Scandinavian Historic Flight

'Old Crow'
Pilot: *John Romain*
Operator:
Scandinavian Historic Flight

'Glam Glen & Old Crow'
Pilots: *G Honbarrier/*
Bud Anderson
Operator:
Gary Honbarrier

'Glam Glen & Old Crow'
Pilots: *C Yeager/Bud Anderson*
Operator:
G Honbarrier/J Roush

'Frenesi'
Pilot: *Jim Beasley, Jr*
Operator:
Jim Beasley, Jr

'Ace of Clubs'
Pilot: *Dan Vance*
Operator
Art Vance

'Isabel III'
Pilot: *Tom Middleton*
Operator:
NZ Fighter Pilots Museum

'Hurry Home Honey'
Pilot: *Brad Hood*
Operator:
C Osborne/Vintage Fighters

'Detroit Miss'
Pilot: *Andy Gent*
Operator:
Scandinavian Historic Flight

For Norman Lees - Mustang pilot, friend and inspiration. . . .

INDEX